Contents

LD

Introduction

Learner Driving programme of driving lessons

D1342469

Contents - continued

Overview

The Driving Skills Workbook is designed to help make the process of learning to drive as easy and as efficient as possible.

The book provides an ideal learning aid to anyone taking professional tuition, or indeed, tuition from a family member or friend. It provides a comprehensive training plan for you and your trainer to follow - The Learner Driving tuition system. By following this system you can be assured of making rapid progress towards your goal of passing the driving test.

The Learner Driving tuition system

The Learner Driving tuition system is made up of a series of carefully planned lessons. Each driving lesson is designed to meet certain learning objectives. The lessons build up your driving skill naturally in small easy steps. The Learner Driving tuition system is split into three parts:

Part 1 - Basic control skills lessons

This part will give you the basic control skills needed to drive safely. This is the starting point for most people and essential if you have no previous driving experience.

Part 2 - Road skills lessons

This part will give you the driving skills that you will need in order to cope with modern road systems.

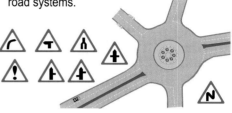

Part 3 - Traffic skills lessons

This part teaches you how to use your basic control and road skills to deal with a wide range of traffic conditions and situations.

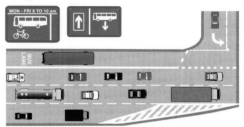

Lesson Content

For each lesson in the programme you will find the following workbook sections:

Introduction

At the start of each lesson you will find an introduction that will state the purpose of the lesson and how it links to the previous lesson or programme as a whole.

Lesson Objectives

This section will summarize the main learning objectives of the lesson.

Subject brief

The workbook contains all the essential information you need to develop your driving skill. This takes the form of a series of subject briefs.

By studying the subject brief beforehand you will save a lot of time in the car on pre-practice explanations. A set of subject briefs are also available on DVD to accompany this programme called "The Driving Skills DVD".

Lesson quiz

To help reinforce your knowledge and understanding of the subject prior to each driving lesson the workbook also provides a series of thought provoking quizzes. Complete each lesson quiz and check your answers. Note any questions incorrectly answered and discuss these with your instructor when you next meet. **Remember to bring the workbook with you** so your instructor can review any questions incorrectly answered and help you update your lesson targets.

Lesson targets

The workbook contains a set of practical targets for each lesson. These targets provide direction to the training and show you precisely what you need to do to prove you have mastered that lesson and every step within it.

Progress monitor

On page 191 you will find the main progress monitor. Use this to record your progress through the training programme.

Theory Test

To complement this skills training programme we also offer a workbook and a CD-Rom to prepare you for the theory test entitled "The Theory Test Highway Code Workbook ...made it easy" and "The Driving Test 3in1 CD-Rom" respectively.

If you wish to purchase any of these additional learning aids you can either visit our website at www.learnerdriving.com or contact our Material Sales department on 01977 691810.

Lesson 1 - Getting moving

Introduction

Before you can begin to learn to drive you must make sure you have a valid provisional driving licence and are physically fit. The main legal requirement in respect to the latter is your eyesight. You must be able to read a car number plate at a distance of 20.5 metres – about 66 feet or 5 car lengths – with glasses or contact lenses, if normally worn. The main aim of the first lesson is to get you driving. However, before this can happen you will need to know about the main controls of the vehicle, what pre-driving checks are necessary, and finally how to move off and stop.

Lesson objectives

By the end of lesson 1 you should be able to:

- ► enter and leave the car safely;
- ► name, and explain the function of the main hand and foot controls;
- ► complete the necessary pre-driving checks;
- ► make the appropriate observation checks before moving off and stopping;
- ► move away safely and under control, making proper use of the accelerator, clutch and handbrake;
- ► use the indicator switch and understand the basic use of direction indicators when moving off and stopping;
- ► use the MSM routine when stopping.

Subject brief

Your first lesson will cover the function of the controls, pre-start comfort and safety (the cockpit drill), precautions before starting the engine, moving off and stopping.

The main controls

The first controls that you need to learn about are the 'main' foot and hand controls.

The accelerator pedal

The accelerator or gas pedal is used with the right foot to control the speed of the car by increasing or decreasing the flow of fuel to the engine. This occurs when the car is in gear and the clutch plates are together. The pedal requires very little pressure to operate and should be used very lightly.

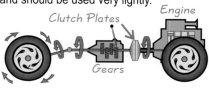

Clutch Plates · Engine · Gears

The foot brake

The foot brake operates brakes on all four wheels and is used to slow the car down. This is operated by swivelling the right foot from the accelerator pedal to the foot brake while trying to keep your heel on the floor. The pedal should be pressed progressively harder then as you reach the required speed smoothly released (i.e. squeeze and ease).

When you press this pedal the brake lights (on the back of the car) come on to warn other drivers that you are slowing down or stopping.

Weight

The clutch

The clutch is used with the left foot to break the link between the engine and the wheels by separating the clutch plates.

You will use it when changing gear and stopping. To operate the pedal you press it firmly as far as it will go and then release it slowly and smoothly.

The handbrake

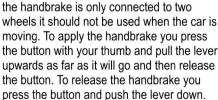

The handbrake is used to hold the car still after it has stopped. Because the handbrake is only connected to two wheels it should not be used when the car is moving. To apply the handbrake you press the button with your thumb and pull the lever upwards as far as it will go and then release the button. To release the handbrake you press the button and push the lever down.

The gear lever

The gear lever is used (with the clutch) to select the gears.

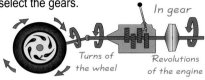

In gear

Turns of the wheel

Revolutions of the engine

The gears determine the number of engine revolutions per turn of the wheel. The higher the number (and therefore the lower the gear) the greater the pulling power, but the slower the speed.

There are usually five forward gears and one reverse gear. Between the gears there is a central position called neutral, when the lever is in this position, no gear is selected.

In neutral

The steering wheel

The steering wheel is used to turn the front wheels when changing direction. You should normally hold the wheel with your hands in the 'ten to two position'. Most control is gained when the 'pull and push' method is used to turn the wheel. (Steering is dealt with in more detail in Lesson 3.)

The indicators

The indicator switch is usually located on a 'stalk' to the left or right of the steering wheel. The switch is designed for fingertip control. To signal that you wish to turn left or right you simply move the switch in the same direction as the steering wheel turns for the manoeuvre.

The cockpit drill

The cockpit drill is a simple sequence of actions that must be carried out each time that you sit behind the driving wheel. However, before you start this drill make sure the car is secure by checking that the handbrake is on.

DOORS: Make sure that all the doors are firmly shut. Take special care if you are carrying children.

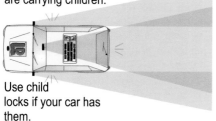

Use child locks if your car has them.

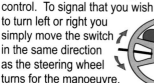

SEAT: Adjust the base of your seat so that you can operate the foot pedals easily. Ensure that you can fully depress the clutch pedal while not over stretching your left leg. If the base of the seat can be raised up and down adjust it until you can get a good view of the road ahead.

Adjust the backrest of your seat so that you can reach all of the steering wheel with your arms slightly bent. When adjusting the back of your seat, make sure that the 'head restraint' is adjusted correctly to protect your neck.

MIRRORS: Adjust all of your mirrors so that you can obtain a clear view of the road behind and to the side of your vehicle. Use your left hand to adjust the interior mirror and be careful not to touch the surface of the mirrors with your fingers. If the vehicle is new to you check which, if any, mirrors are convex (i.e. curved to give a wider field of vision).

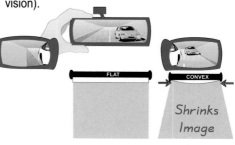

SEATBELTS: Fasten your seatbelt and make sure that your passengers fasten theirs. The driver is responsible for seatbelt wearing by children under 14 years of age. Full details about seatbelt laws can be found in The Highway Code.

Moving off

Moving off is easy so long as you follow a basic routine. Once you have started the engine and prepared the car for moving you use the Mirrors-Signal-Manouevre routine to move away.

Starting the engine

Before starting the engine you should check that the handbrake is on and that the gear lever is in neutral. Turn the ignition key and immediately release it as the engine starts (to avoid damaging the starter motor).

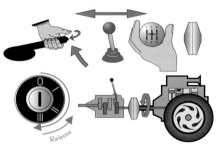

Get the car ready to move (Prepare)

1. Press the clutch down as far as it will go.

2. Select first gear.

3. Rest your left hand on the handbrake.

4. 'Set the power'. Press the accelerator pedal slightly until the engine makes a lively humming sound and then hold it still. You are trying to generate sufficient power to move the car once the handbrake is released and the clutch pedal is up.

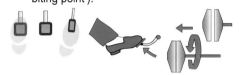

5. Bring the clutch up until the sound of the engine drops slightly and then keep both feet still (this is called the clutch 'biting point').

Mirrors, Signal (Observe)

1. Check your mirrors in one of the following sequences:
Left (nearside) door mirror, interior mirror, right (offside) door mirror or; interior mirror, left door mirror, right door mirror. Is it safe to proceed?

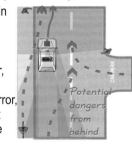

2. Look over your right shoulder to check your offside blind-spot. Is it still safe to proceed?

3. Signal, if anyone will benefit and return your hand to the handbrake.

Manoeuvre (Move)

1. When you are sure that it is safe to move, release the handbrake.
2. Bring the clutch up smoothly all the way as you gently press the accelerator to get the car to move forward.
3. As you begin to move check your mirrors again.
4. Move your left foot away from the clutch pedal and rest it on the floor.
5. Steer to your normal driving position, about a metre from the kerb.
6. Switch off the signal, if applied.
7. Press the gas pedal to pick up speed and look well ahead.

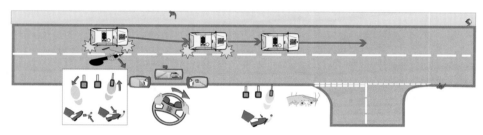

Stopping

Apply the Mirrors-Signal-Manoeuvre routine for stopping. Check your mirrors to ensure it is safe, signal if it will benefit anyone. Steer closer, but parallel to the kerb. Press the foot brake progressively harder and just before the car stops begin to ease off (squeeze and ease) and then depress the clutch pedal fully down just before you stop. Finally, make the car safe; apply the handbrake, select neutral, remove your feet from the pedals and cancel the signal, if necessary.

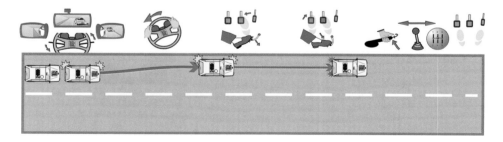

Lesson quiz

1. On the diagram below please indicate which pedal(s) are operated by the right foot (R) and which are operated by the left (L). Also indicate which is called the accelerator or gas (A), which is called the foot brake (B) and which is called the clutch (C).

Foot (L / R) ☐ ☐ ☐

Name (A / B / C) ☐ ☐ ☐

2. The accelerator pedal: (Tick as appropriate.)

True   False

☐   ☐   Is a "go faster" pedal.

☐   ☐   Should be depressed very slowly and smoothly.

☐   ☐   Controls the rate of fuel fed to the engine and therefore the revolutions of the engine.

☐   ☐   Can cause the car to speed up or slow down when one of the gears is engaged and the clutch plates are together.

3. Mark two crosses on the wheel to show the position of your hands when driving forwards.

4. The indicator switch is on the left-hand side of this steering wheel.
    Write '1' or '2' in the box below to show which way you
    would move the switch in order to signal
    to the left.

    Which?

    1

    2

5. The foot brake pedal:

    Weight

    True   False

    ☐   ☐   Should be pressed progressively harder.

    ☐   ☐   Operates the brakes on all four wheels.

    ☐   ☐   Operates the red lights at the back.

6. The clutch pedal:

    True   False

    ☐   ☐   Should be pressed
                  firmly to the floor before engaging (i.e. selecting) a gear.

    ☐   ☐   Should be released very quickly.

    ☐   ☐   Should be released smoothly and carefully.

11

7. Link the clutch plate diagram with the appropriate circumstance. Please match the letter denoting the circumstance, to the appropriate diagram.

A) Engine on,
   Gear engaged,
   Clutch pedal up

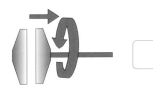

B) Engine off,
   Gear in neutral,
   Clutch pedal up

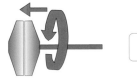

C) Engine on,
   Gear engaged,
   Clutch pedal down

D) Engine off,
   Gear engaged,
   Clutch pedal down

8. When the gear stick is in neutral and your foot is not on the clutch pedal the clutch plates are apart.

True ☐   False ☐

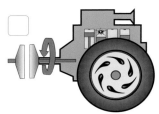

9. The cockpit drill is the safety drill that you must carry out:

Every time you sit behind the wheel of a car. ☐

Only after someone else has been driving the car. ☐

Occasionally. ☐

10. Draw or shade the area behind the vehicle below that you should be able to see in each of the mirrors assuming that the mirrors have been properly adjusted.

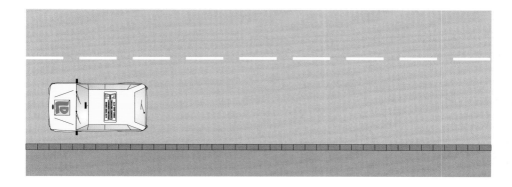

11. Which hand should you normally use to adjust the interior mirror?

The left hand. ☐

The right hand. ☐

12. Often door mirrors are convex rather than flat this gives a wider field of vision but it makes objects seem:

☐ Smaller and therefore further away.

☐ Larger and therefore closer.

13. Tick the boxes to show which of the statements below is true and which is false.

	True	False
When fitted, seatbelts must be worn by all passengers in motor cars.	☐	☐
Seatbelts, if fitted, need not be worn by adults travelling in the rear seats.	☐	☐
The driver is legally responsible for belt wearing by children under the age of 14.	☐	☐
Seatbelts reduce the risk of serious injury in an accident.	☐	☐

14. It is important to release the ignition key as soon as you hear the engine start. This is because:

The starter motor might otherwise be damaged. ☐

If you don't, you will use too much fuel. ☐

The engine will stall if you don't release the key. ☐

15. What advice does The Highway Code give about signal use?

Give signals every time you change position. ☐

Signals must only be given by using the indicators. ☐

Give signals to help or warn other road users. ☐

16. According to The Highway Code when should you consult your mirrors?

☐ Frequently to see what's behind.

☐ Before changing direction or position.

☐ Before signalling.

☐ Before changing speed.

☐ Before doing anything.

You should also consult your mirrors before opening the car doors.

True ☐   False ☐

17. The Highway Code states that you should:

Normally drive just left of the centre line. ☐

Normally keep to the left. ☐

Normally keep close to the side of the road. ☐

18. 'Setting the gas' requires you to: (Tick two items.)

☐ Press the accelerator pedal fully down.

☐ Press the accelerator to generate sufficient engine power to move the car forward once the handbrake is released and the clutch pedal is up.

☐ Press the accelerator until you can hear a lively humming sound.

19. The clutch 'biting point' is fully achieved when: (Tick two items.)

☐ The clutch pedal is fully up.

☐ The clutch plates begin to bite and transfer power to the wheels.

☐ The engine tone dips.

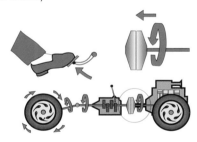

20. Draw a line to represent the path you would need the gear lever to take in order to select first gear assuming it is currently in neutral.

To ensure that the engine didn't stall you would first need to fully depress the ⬚ pedal.

21. Please number the steps for starting the engine.

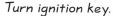

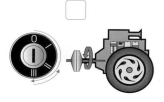

Turn ignition key.   *Gear in Neutral.*   *Handbrake on.*

22. Please number the steps for preparing the car to move.

Select first gear.   *Clutch to biting point.*   *Set the gas.*

23. Please number the steps for making the appropriate observational checks before moving off. Mirrors-

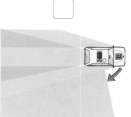

Left door mirror. *Right door mirror.*   *Central mirror.*

Right blind spot.

24. Please number the final steps for moving away.
Signal-Manoeuvre

Handbrake off.

Signal, if necessary.

Slowly clutch fully up and a bit more gas.

More gas to pick up speed.

Steer to normal driving position.

Signal off.

Additional mirrors check.

25. Please number the steps for stopping.

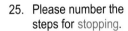

Steer towards and parallel to kerb

Brake progressively.

Mirrors: interior and left.

Signal off.

Signal, if necessary.

Clutch down.

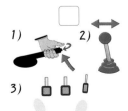

1)   2)
3)

Make car safe.

26. Complete the diagram below for moving off.

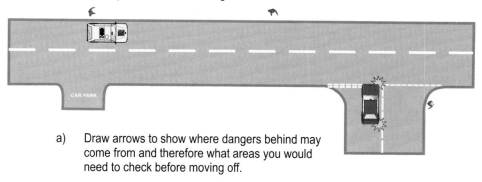

a) Draw arrows to show where dangers behind may come from and therefore what areas you would need to check before moving off.

b) Draw two lines to show the path of the front wheels of the car as it moves away.

c) Looking at question 24; use the step numbers to show at which points on the cars path the last 4 steps would approximately occur on the above diagram.

27. Complete the diagram below for stopping.

a) Assuming you have just decided to pull up on the left at point A draw two lines to show the path of the front wheels of the car as it pulls up.

b) Looking at question 25; use the step numbers to show at which points on the cars path these steps approximately occur.

Lesson targets

Clutch Control ✔
MSM Routine ✔
...ination ✔

At the end of the lesson tick those targets below that have been achieved. If any of the targets are ticked as completed with help, review them again after your next lesson.

Getting ready to drive

With help from my instructor | Without help from my instructor

I can read a number plate from the minimum required distance (20.5 metres, about 5 car lengths).

 1

I can complete a cockpit drill.

2 2

I can locate, and know how to use, the main controls.

3 3

Moving off and stopping

When moving off from the side of the road I:

Can make the necessary checks, release the steering lock and start the engine safely.

4 4

Prepare to move off safely.

5 5

Make correct observation checks and signal as appropriate.

6 6

Move away smoothly and take up the normal driving position.

7 7

When stopping on the left-hand side of the road I:

Make the correct observation checks and signal as appropriate.

8 8

Use the foot brake and clutch correctly.

9 9

Secure the car after I have stopped.

10 10

Lesson 2 - Gears

Introduction

Having mastered moving off in a straight line, you now need to learn how to change gear in order to make progress as you drive along.

Smooth gear changing is the first of three key foundation skills that you will need to learn. The others being steering and clutch control. These three foundation skills form the basis of most if not all the road, traffic and reversing skills covered in the other parts of the Learner Driving programme. Therefore before you move onto part 2 of the programme it is vitally important that these three foundation skills become second nature to you – an automatic response requiring little or no conscious thought. This is why the next three lessons are dedicated to the development of these most important skills. Taking the time to concentrate on them at this early stage will dramatically speed up your progress later on.

Lesson objectives

By the end of lesson 2 you should be able to:

▶ make upward gear changes, in sequence, 1 through to 5;

▶ make downward gear changes, in sequence, 5 through to 1;

▶ make upward selective gear changes from 2 to 4 and 3 to 5;

▶ make downward selective gear changes from 5 to 2, 5 to 3, 5 to 1 , 4 to 2 , 4 to 1 and 3 to 1;

▶ maintain a straight course and look well ahead whilst changing gear.

Subject Brief

During this lesson you will learn how to make the car go faster by using the gears to reduce the number of engine revolutions per turn of the wheel. This will allow you to increase the speed of the car but it will reduce its pulling power.

Gear	Power	Speed	MPH
1	High	Low	0-10
2			10-25
3			20-40
4			30-50
5	Low	High	40-70
R	High	Low	0-5

Gears can be changed up or down. This has nothing to do with the direction that you move the gear lever. It simply means that you change to a high gear (4 or 5) or a low gear (1 or 2).

The basic rule is that you change up through the gears as the speed of the car increases

and down when you need more power from the engine. For example, you would change down when climbing a hill or pulling away at low speed.

The basic gear changing rule is 'gears to go - brakes to slow'. As the car increases speed, change up through the gears. When you want to slow down, use the foot brake. You need only change to a lower gear when you need the accelerator again to 'drive' the car along.

This means that you may sometimes miss out gears. For example, by changing from fifth or fourth gear to second gear. This method is called 'selective' or 'block' gear changing. There are also times when you might selectively change up, having used a lower gear for better acceleration or more pulling power followed by a change to fifth gear when you have reached your intended cruising speed.

Procedure for changing gear

The actual sequence for changing gear is as follows:

1. Firstly, make sure that it is safe to change gear. Any place where it was necessary to use both hands to steer the car such as a corner or bend would not be suitable.

2. Secondly, you need to ease off the accelerator pedal just prior to or as you depress the clutch pedal. The two actions are almost simultaneous.

This will dramatically reduce the power being transmitted from the engine to the gearbox, thus enabling you to select a gear without causing any damage to the gear mechanism.

3. Thirdly, you select gears using your left hand while being careful to look ahead and not at the gear knob.

When selecting 1st gear you would normally cup your hand with your palm away from you in this way.

When selecting 2nd or 4th gear from the 1st, 3rd or 5th gear position you would usually place the palm of your hand away from you in this manner.

If however you wanted to change from 2nd gear to 4th gear or visa-versa you would cup your hand with your palm towards you as shown.

4. Fourthly, with your left foot, you would release the clutch pedal in one smooth action just prior to reapplying pressure to the accelerator pedal with your right foot. Again the two actions are almost simultaneous.

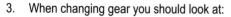

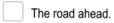

Lesson 2 - Gears

Lesson quiz

1. Number the boxes to show the correct sequence of actions that you would carry out in order to change gear.

   Press gas pedal ☐

   Press the clutch down ☐

   Move the gear lever ☐

   Ease off the gas pedal ☐

   Let the clutch up ☐

2. Number the gear positions (1-5) on the gear knob right.

3. When changing gear you should look at:

   ☐ The gear lever.

   ☐ The road ahead.

   ☐ Your feet.

4. The gears are numbered 1, 2, 3, 4 and 5. Is it always necessary to use them in this order?

   Yes ☐   No ☐

5. In the table below roughly indicate the speed range in miles per hour for each of the gears. For example first gear should be 0 - 10.

	POWER (Revs. per wheel turn)	SPEED	MPH
1	Max	Min	0-10
2			
3			
4			
5	Min	Max	
R	Max	Min	

Lesson targets

At the end of the lesson tick those targets below that have been achieved. If any of the targets are ticked as completed with help, review them again after your next lesson.

Changing gear

When changing gear I:

	With help from my instructor	Without help from my instructor
Look well ahead, not at the gear lever.	1	1
Smoothly co-ordinate hand and foot movements.	2	2
Hold the gear lever correctly.	3	3

Practice changes

I have practised and am able to complete the following gear changes:

	With help	Without help
First through to fifth.	4	4
Fifth through to first.	5	5
Block changes down.	6	6
Block changes up.	7	7

Lesson 3 - Steering

Introduction

Having mastered the first key foundation skill in lesson 2 it is time to move onto the next in lesson 3 - steering. While it is relatively easy to make slight steering adjustments many manoeuvres require you to turn the car sharply to either the left or to the right. To do this effectively you will need to learn the "pull-push" method of steering.

Again, as with all foundation skills, it is vital that this skill becomes second nature to you, hence, the reason why the whole of lesson 3 is dedicated to this most important skill.

Lesson Objectives

By the end of this lesson you should able to:

- ► use the "look where you want the car to go" method of staying on course;
- ► use the 'pull-push' steering method to complete the following car-park exercises
  - ► sharp turns to the left,
  - ► sharp turns to the right,
  - ► u-turns,
  - ► figure of eight turns;
- ► steer accurately when moving off, passing obstructions, and turning corners.

Subject brief

During this lesson you will learn how to keep your car on course and use the pull-push method of steering to turn corners. What is probably the most important rule about steering may not seem obvious. It is that you not only steer with your hands, but also with your eyes! You do this by looking where you want to go. This tells your brain what to do with your hands. Your peripheral vision (i.e. your vision to each side) helps you to keep your road position.

Pull - push method of steering

This method ensures that you keep both hands in contact with the wheel at all times and that the wheel is never allowed to spin out of control. Once the wheels are fully turned left or right this is known as full lock.

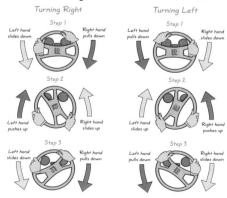

25

Lesson quiz

1. The diagram below shows the path taken by the front wheels of a car as it turns a corner. Draw two lines to show the path that you think the rear wheels will take.

Now place an 'X' in one of the boxes to show the uppermost point that a traffic cone could be placed, without being hit by the turning car.

2. You can tell precisely which way the wheels are pointing by looking at the steering wheel.

   True ☐   *False* ☐

3. To keep the car on course you should look at:

   Where you want the car to go.   ☐
   The centre white line.   ☐
   The kerb.   ☐

4. Peripheral vision helps you to see;

☐ to the front?   **or**   ☐ to the sides?

It plays a vital role with positioning and negotiating small gaps.

True ☐   *False* ☐

5. What is full lock in regard to steering? Is it:

One turn of the steering wheel.   ☐

When you cannot turn the steering wheel any further in a particular direction.   ☐

When you hold the steering wheel tightly and lock your arms.   ☐

6. When driving forward you must hold the steering wheel with both hands unless operating another control or using a hand signal.

☐ True

☐ False

Lesson targets

At the end of the lesson tick those targets below that have been achieved. If any of the targets are ticked as completed with help, review them again after your next lesson.

Steering

When steering the car I:

	With help from my instructor	Without help from my instructor
Look well ahead, not at the controls.	1	1
Use the pull-push method.	2	2
Keep the car under full control.	3	3

Steering practice

During the steering lesson with my instructor I:

	With help from my instructor	Without help from my instructor
Steered accurately when moving off.	4	4
Steered safely around parked cars.	5	5
Steered using full left-hand and right-hand lock on a deserted road or a car park.	6	6
Followed a suitable road position.	7	7

Minor Controls

I can locate and operate all of the minor controls of the car.	8	8

Lesson 4 - Co-ordination

Introduction

In lesson 4 you will further develop the skills introduced in the first three lessons paying particular attention to your clutch control - the third foundation skill. As with the other foundation skills of steering and gear changing the more attention you pay to the development of it at this early stage the faster you will progress later on.

Lesson objectives

By the end of this lesson you should be able to:

► control the clutch smoothly and accurately;

► hold the car on the clutch on various uphill gradients;

► maintain a crawling pace uphill, downhill and on the flat;

► move off uphill;

► move off downhill;

► move off at an angle;

► negotiate some basic junctions with full support;

► use the MSM routine when overtaking stationary vehicles;

► check mirrors before changing speed, position or direction and give appropriate signals when required;

► correctly answer questions about use of mirrors and signals.

Subject brief

As soon as you have mastered the basic skills of moving off on the level, changing gear and steering, you can use them to help with some slightly more complex manoeuvres. During this lesson you will learn how to move off uphill, down hill and at an angle from behind a parked vehicle. You will also learn how to overtake stationary vehicles and improve your mirror and signal use.

Moving off stage 2

Uphill

Use more gas when setting the gas. This will give you the power needed to move away uphill slowly and smoothly. Release the handbrake gently. If the car rolls back, bring the clutch up a little more.

Downhill

No gas! Let gravity do the hard work for you. Control the speed with the foot brake bringing the clutch up gently as soon as possible. The steeper the gradient the higher the gear you should start in.

At an angle

You may need a signal, even if you think there is no-one to benefit. When moving off at an angle it is harder to see and be seen. Check your blind spot at least twice. Because you are moving off slowly, other vehicles may approach. Use clutch-control to keep your speed down until you

have straightened your wheels.

Mirror use

When using the mirrors you have to be careful not to take your eyes off the road ahead for too long. Use quick glances and minimal head movement. Register what you see. Are there any vehicles behind or to the side? How fast are they travelling? How close are they? Are they signalling? Once you have collected this information consider whether they will affect you and whether you need to take any action. As a minimum you need to know this before you change (or signal your intention to change) the cars position, direction or speed. If you are stationary you also need to know this before you open the car doors.

Below are some examples showing you why you need to use your mirrors frequently and certainly before signalling or changing the cars position, direction or speed.

*Before
signalling*

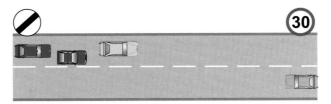

*Before
increasing
speed*

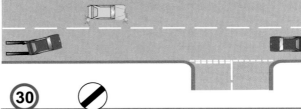

*Before
reducing
speed*

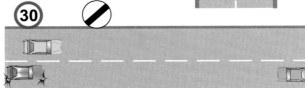

*Before
changing
position*

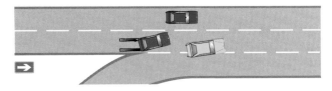

Signal use

Horn

Signals should only be used to help or warn other road users (including pedestrians) of your intended actions or your presence. If other road users will not benefit from a signal then a signal may not be necessary. See The Highway Code for the precise meaning of all these signals. Timing your signal is important. Too early and it may be misleading. Too late and other road users may not see or hear it, or have time to react to it. Signals can also be given by hand as shown below:

Meeting and overtaking stationary vehicles

When you approach stationary vehicles use the Mirrors-Signal-Manoeuvre routine. Check your mirrors to see if it is safe to give a signal and if so determine whether it would benefit anyone. Move out to just left of the centre of the road to gain a better view of any oncoming traffic. If you cannot overtake the stationary vehicles without affecting any oncoming traffic slow down and be prepared to stop just left of the centre of the road about two car lengths from the rear of the stationary vehicle.

Maintain adequate clearance throughout; about a metre away, if possible.

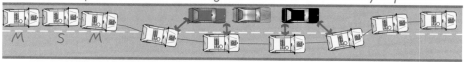

On busy housing estates you can sometimes be confronted with the problem of meeting traffic head on where it is difficult to determine who has priority or where your view is very restricted or where the gap you intend to proceed through is very narrow. Anticipation and common courtesy play an important role.

Try to ensure that you are seen and if possible obtain eye contact with the other road users. Assess the speed and distance of the approaching vehicle. If you are confident that you will arrive earlier than the oncoming vehicle it is likely that the other driver will give you priority but don't assume it. Keep observing the other drivers actions carefully. The narrower the gap and the more pedestrians that are about the slower your speed should be.

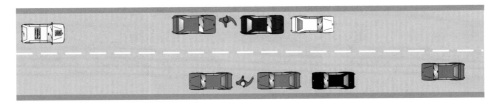

Passing places

On single track roads you will often find passing places to allow oncoming vehicles to pass. If the passing place is on your left hand side then you would normally wait in the passing place area. If it is on your right hand side you would normally wait opposite the passing place in such a position that the oncoming vehicle could move into the passing place area.

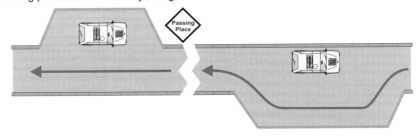

Traffic calming measures

In housing estates it is becoming more common to find various types of traffic calming measures. The most common one is referred to as the "sleeping policeman". This is simply a hump in the road. Normally the speed limit in such an area would be 20 mph or less.

You may also find other types of traffic calming measures such as extended causeways. These can be treated in much the same way as a parked car.

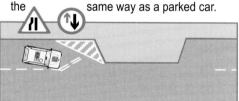

Mini Roundabout

The mini-roundabout is also becoming a common feature in housing estates as a traffic calming device. Although you will cover roundabouts later in some detail your instructor may need to cover the basics at this stage. At mini-roundabouts you give way to traffic approaching from the right.

Wait

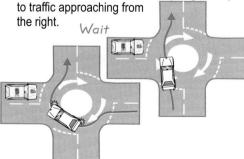

However, you may proceed if you are sure the vehicle from the right is turning into your road as shown below:

Proceed

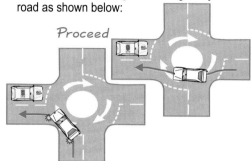

Lesson quiz

1. When moving off from behind a parked vehicle, you will usually need to look around, over your right shoulder, more than once.

   True ☐   False ☐

2. Listed below are a series of signals that might be used by other drivers. Please match the letter, denoting the meaning of the signal, to the appropriate signal description shown.

 ☐

A) This sound warns others of your presence and is particularly useful when other road users cannot see you.

 ☐

B) These lights indicate that the car in front is slowing down or stopping.

 ☐

C) These flashing lights are used to warn others in front of you of your presence. When acting on this signal never assume that it is a signal to proceed use your own judgement and proceed carefully.

 ☐

D) When all four indicator lights are flashing this indicates that the vehicle represents a hazard and extreme caution should be taken.

3. In the diagram below please show where you would position the car before overtaking the stationary vehicles on the left.

4. In question 3 if no vehicles were following you and there were no pedestrians about would you need to signal?

   Yes ☐   No ☐

5. Draw two lines to show the path of the front wheels of the car as you overtake the parked cars on the left (assuming no vehicles were approaching).

6. Before considering a signal to overtake in the above example which mirror or mirrors would you use and in which order ?

   ☐ Interior mirror

   ☐ Nearside (left) door mirror

   ☐ Offside (right) door mirror

7. Place the letter M on the above diagram at the point or points where you think you should use the mirrors.

8. In the example (below) you had to stop to allow oncoming traffic to pass which routine would you use before overtaking the cars?

Lesson targets

At the end of the lesson tick those targets below that have been achieved. If any of the targets are ticked as completed with help, review them again after your next lesson.

Moving off

I can move off smoothly and safely:

With help from my instructor   *Without help from my instructor*

On various uphill gradients.

On various downhill gradients.

From behind a parked vehicle.

1   1

2   2

3   3

Co-ordination

During the co-ordination lesson with my instructor I:

Demonstrated effective clutch control.

Operated all the controls smoothly.

Properly used the MSM routine when overtaking stationary vehicles.

Checked my mirrors when necessary.

Gave signals when required.

Maintained a safe road position and gave adequate clearance to other road users.

4   4

5   5

6   6

7   7

8   8

9   9

Lesson 5 - The emergency stop

Introduction

Before we can move onto busier traffic situations it is very important that you learn how to stop in an emergency - as if a child had, without warning, run out into the road in front of you. A good driver would rarely have to stop in an emergency as he or she would always be on the look out for potentially dangerous situations and act accordingly. Never the less, a situation may arise that could not have been anticipated and consequently your only course of action might be to undertake an emergency stop. Before you go on to developing your skills in locations with more pedestrians and traffic it is vital that you learn this most important skill.

Lesson Objectives

By the end of this lesson you should be able to:

- ► describe the concept of stopping distances, with regard to thinking and braking distance;
- ► complete the emergency stop exercise:
- ► with full steering and braking control, braking progressively;
- ► using the brake and clutch correctly;
- ► securing the car after stopping;
- ► making full and proper observational checks before moving off;
- ► at various speeds;
- ► explain how to correct a skid.

Subject brief

During this lesson you will learn about stopping distances and how to stop in an emergency.

The emergency stop

The key learning points to remember about this exercise are:

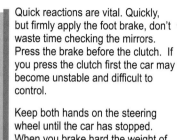

Quick reactions are vital. Quickly, but firmly apply the foot brake, don't waste time checking the mirrors. Press the brake before the clutch. IF you press the clutch first the car may become unstable and difficult to control.

Keep both hands on the steering wheel until the car has stopped. When you brake hard the weight of the car is thrown forwards; this means that you need a firm grip on the steering wheel to maintain direction or correct skids.

Don't try to steer when braking harshly otherwise you may put the car into a skid unless your car is fitted with an anti-locking brake system (ABS).

If the car skids during an emergency stop you should quickly release and re-apply the foot brake. This will allow the tyres to regain their grip on the road surface.

The car can move sideways in a skid. If this happens, concentrate on where you want to go, turning your head, if necessary. Turn the steering wheel the same way as you are looking - towards where you want to go. Remember to release and re-apply the foot brake as you steer!

Take extra observations before moving away checking both blind spots.

37

Speed and stopping distances

The distance it takes to stop a vehicle depends upon the weight, speed, brakes, tyres and suspension of the vehicle. It also depends upon your reaction speed or thinking time and the road surface itself. The Highway Code contains a guide to normal stopping distances assuming a typical dry road surface and average vehicle characteristics. What is less appreciated is the distance you travel per second. Below you can see the distance you would travel in car lengths (i.e. about 4 metres) per second at different speeds.

Distance travelled in car lengths per second at:

30 MPH   3.35 (13.4 metres).

40 MPH   4.47 (17.88 metres).

50 MPH   5.59 (22.36 metres).

60 MPH   6.70 (26.8 metres).

Lesson quiz

1. The average person takes just two thirds (i.e. 0.66) of a second to react and begin to apply the brakes. How far would the car travel (in car lengths or metres) at the following speeds before you could react (i.e. your thinking distance?).

30 MPH	40 MPH	50 MPH	60 MPH

(The Highway Code will help you answer this question)

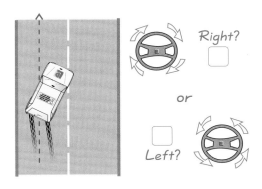

2. Tick the appropriate box to show which way you would turn the steering wheel to correct this skid.

Right?

or

Left?

3. What would be the speed of the car in the diagram below if it needed the following car lengths to stop (i.e. 6 (A), 9 (B) or 13 (C))?

MPH

_____ A

_____ B

_____ C

⬛ = _____ distance   ⬛ = _____ distance

4. On a dry road the quickest and shortest way to stop is to brake to a point just before the wheels lock. Even if the wheels lock it still achieves a high degree of braking but prevents you from being able to steer the car.

True ☐   False ☐

5. Which shoulder or shoulders should you look over before moving off following an emergency stop?

☐ Left   ☐ Right   ☐ Both

6. It is very important to apply the clutch early to avoid stalling the engine when completing an emergency stop.

True ☐   False ☐

Lesson targets

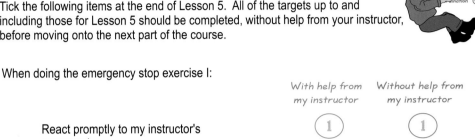

Tick the following items at the end of Lesson 5. All of the targets up to and including those for Lesson 5 should be completed, without help from your instructor, before moving onto the next part of the course.

When doing the emergency stop exercise I:

	With help from my instructor	Without help from my instructor
React promptly to my instructor's command.	1	1
Keep both hands on the steering wheel.	2	2
Use the pedals correctly.	3	3
Stop in a straight line.	4	4
Stop promptly without skidding.	5	5

After I have stopped the car in the emergency stop exercise I:

Secure the car correctly.	6	6
Take a deep breath to relax.	7	7
Check my mirrors and look over both shoulders before moving off.	8	8

Lesson 6 - Hazard drill and basic junctions

Introduction

You should by now be well on the way to perfecting your foundation skills covered in part 1 of the Learner Driving programme. These foundation skills form the basis of most if not all the road, traffic and reversing skills you will learn from this point onwards.

Lesson 6 is the first road skills lesson and covers the basic routine or drill that you will use whenever you negotiate a driving hazard such as a junction. We call this routine the hazard drill.

This drill is based upon a simplified version of the Police System of Vehicle Control. Although this system is normally only taught on advanced driving courses we feel that the basics should be taught to learners and hence the reason for its inclusion in this programme. In this lesson you will be concentrating on using this drill for dealing with simple junctions and other static road hazards found in quiet suburban areas.

Lesson objectives

By the end of this lesson you should be able to:

- ► use the hazard drill on the approach to simple junctions and other static road hazards such as parked vehicles;
- ► safely turn left or right into simple junctions on roads with little or no traffic;
- ► safely cross the path of oncoming vehicles on roads with little traffic;
- ► safely emerge from simple junctions onto roads with little or no traffic;
- ► negotiate more complex junctions with full support or prompting;
- ► understand the term 'hazard' in relationship to driving;
- ► fully understand the need for a routine approach to hazards;
- ► understand why the steps in the hazard drill are considered in a specific order but are not always acted upon.

Subject brief

During this lesson you will learn about a special drill to help you deal with hazards safely. The hazard drill that we use is based on a simplified version of the police system of car control. In this lesson you will learn how to use this drill to approach junctions, and how to use this drill to overtake stationary or slow moving vehicles.

Hazard drill (MSPSG)

Each time you are presented with a potential or actual hazard on the road (i.e. anything that may require you to have to change speed, position or direction) you will go through the hazard drill on the next page one or more times. While each step of the drill needs to be considered in the order shown it need not necessarily be acted upon.

Hazard Drill (MSPSG)

MIRRORS
(Must)

Use your interior mirror and side mirror(s) early. Glance into your right and left blind spots as appropriate. Repeat as necessary at any stage in the drill.

SIGNAL
(Surely)

Give signals in good time. Use signals to help or warn other road users. Be careful not to give misleading signals.

POSITION
(Prevent)

Determine the best position/course to negotiate the hazard. Think before you change position; be careful not to mislead others.

SPEED
(Some)

Adjust your speed so that you can negotiate the hazard ahead and stop within the distance you can see to be clear.

GEAR
(Grief)

Select the gear to match your speed and the power you need. Make sure that the gear is selected before the hazard is negotiated.

Turning into a side road

The hazard drill is effectively used at least twice when you wish to turn left or right from a main road into a side road. Once on the approach and once following the turn.

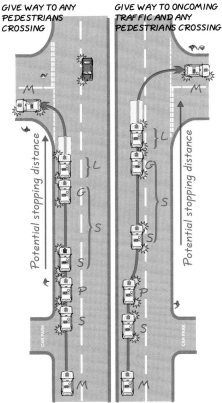

GIVE WAY TO ANY PEDESTRIANS CROSSING

GIVE WAY TO ONCOMING TRAFFIC AND ANY PEDESTRIANS CROSSING

Because of the importance of taking observations before you turn instructors often add an extra step called Look and amalgamate the gear step into Speed. In this event the hazard drill becomes the approach routine MSPSL. If you follow this routine please note that you take observations to the rear, sides and ahead as necessary throughout the routine and not just at the end.

The key learning points are as follows:

1. Signal early, but be careful not to mislead others into thinking you are turning earlier than intended. Because it is usually impossible to determine whether other road users will benefit from a signal (particularly road users in the side road) you should always signal when turning at road junctions.

2. If the potential stopping distance to the turning point is not sufficient for your current speed you will need to reduce speed before you signal and change position. Consequently, use the hazard drill twice on approach in this situation.

3. When turning left you would normally position your car as close to the left as it was safe to do so being careful to maintain adequate clearance from any pedestrians near the edge of the road. Do not overtake any cyclists, motorcyclists or horse riders immediately before your turning. When turning right you would normally position the vehicle just left of the centre of the road (or in the area of the road marked for right turning traffic) provided sufficient room was available for oncoming vehicles to pass safely; otherwise you would keep to the left.

4. As you reduce speed in preparation to turn you will need to assess which gear you should select to complete the turn if it is not necessary to give way or stop. Your own skill, the angle of the turn, the width and gradient of the side road and what you can see of the road into which you want to turn will all need to be considered. Basically you continue to reduce speed until you are certain that you can safely negotiate the turn; then at that point select the gear that matches your speed.

5. When turning left or right you must give way to any pedestrians crossing the face of the junction. Stop just before the point where you would start to turn if you cannot get the whole of your vehicle into the side road safely. Plan to stop but look to go.

6. When turning left you have priority over oncoming traffic turning right into the side road. However, when you are turning right oncoming traffic has priority over you so you must wait for a gap in the traffic. Again you would wait just before the point at which you would turn.

Naturally, once you have stopped the gap needed to cross the road safely will need to be bigger as you are starting from a standstill position. Therefore you should try to time your approach to coincide with any oncoming gaps that are of a suitable size to allow you to cross.

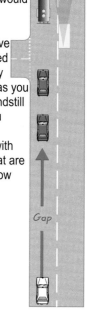

7. If you find that you have to wait; stop just before the point where you would start to turn and select first gear and be ready to move. If you have to wait for a while you should apply your handbrake (if not already applied) and select neutral. Watch for a gap and get ready to move as it approaches; check your mirrors and then turn if it is safe to do so.

8. You may require additional mirror checks on your approach if it is particularly long or if the road is very busy. When turning left you need to particularly supplement the use of your interior mirror with the left hand door mirror and when turning right with the right hand door mirror. If you find yourself in a queue of traffic use all three mirrors.

Emerging from a side road

The approach routine when you wish to emerge from a side road onto the major road is the same as when you want to turn into a side road.

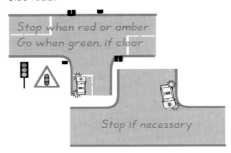

Stop when red or amber
Go when green, if clear

Stop if necessary

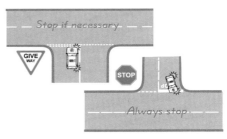

Stop if necessary

GIVE WAY

STOP

Always stop

However, extra consideration needs to be given before you emerge into the major road. In particular, vehicles on the major road have priority over you therefore you may need to slow down or stop to allow them to pass before you emerge.

Observations on approach are critical to determine whether you can emerge without stopping and in which gear. Some junctions are open allowing you to take early observations. Others are closed restricting your view.

OPEN

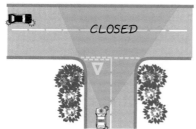

CLOSED

Overtaking slow and stationary vehicles

The overtaking manoeuvre requires you to employ the hazard drill at least three times. Once as part of the preparation to overtake, once as part of the actual overtake and once as you return back to the left side of the road.

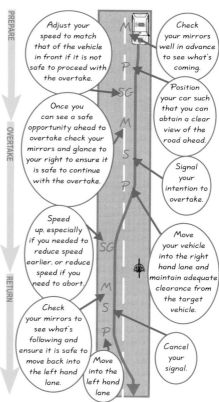

PREPARE

Adjust your speed to match that of the vehicle in front if it is not safe to proceed with the overtake.

Check your mirrors well in advance to see what's coming.

Position your car such that you can obtain a clear view of the road ahead.

OVERTAKE

Once you can see a safe opportunity ahead to overtake check your mirrors and glance to your right to ensure it is safe to continue with the overtake.

Signal your intention to overtake.

Move your vehicle into the right hand lane and maintain adequate clearance from the target vehicle.

RETURN

Speed up, especially if you needed to reduce speed earlier, or reduce speed if you need to abort.

Check your mirrors to see what's following and ensure it is safe to move back into the left hand lane.

Move into the left hand lane

Cancel your signal.

45

Lesson quiz

1. List the first letter of each element of the hazard drill:

2. In the example below, assuming there is no traffic behind, and that there are no pedestrians around would you need to signal your intention to move off?

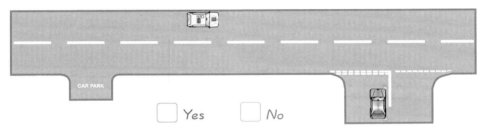

☐ Yes   ☐ No

3. In the example below assuming that no vehicles are driving towards you and that you are proceeding ahead would you need to signal right to show the traffic behind that you intended to overtake the red car parked on the left?

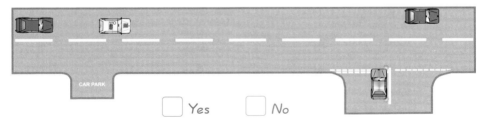

☐ Yes   ☐ No

4. In the situation below draw two lines to show the path of the front wheels of the car as it overtakes the green car parked on the left.

On the line place the first letter of each item of the hazard drill as you would potentially consider or apply it.

5. In the diagram below indicate when you would signal and where you would make mirror checks in your interior and right (offside) door mirror. Write the letter 'S' to denote when you would signal and the letter 'M' when you would make mirror checks.

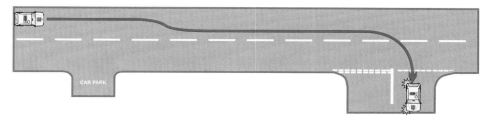

6. In the diagram below indicate when you would signal and where you would make mirror checks in your interior and left (nearside) door mirror. Write the letter 'S' to denote when you would signal and the letter 'M' when you would make mirror checks.

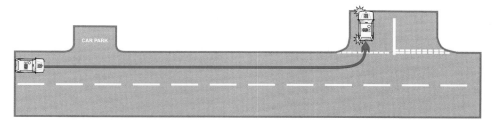

7. When using the hazard drill.

Why can't you:

● Signal before using your mirrors?

● Move into position before you signal?

● Reduce speed before you move into position?

● Change gear before you reduce speed?

Consider the above and discuss your thoughts with your instructor.

8. What factors below would you consider when determining the speed and gear you will need when approaching to turn left or right into a side road? If it applies to turning left only use 'L', right only use 'R' or 'B' if it applies to both or if it is not relevant leave it blank.

Your own ability to negotiate the turning.

The weight of the car and the depth of your tyre tread.

The angle of the corner or the turn.

The width and the gradient of the side road.

What you can see of the road you are turning into.

The presence of pedestrians on the corner.

The height of the kerb.

The speed and distance of oncoming traffic.

9. Assuming that there were no oncoming vehicles which gear would you probably use to negotiate the following right turns 1st or 2nd gear?

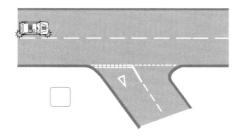 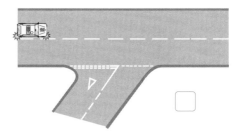

10. Looking at the road layouts below which gear would you probably need to negotiate the following left turns. 1st, 2nd or 3rd gear?

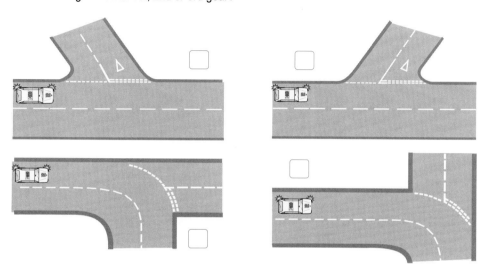

11. If you could see that a vehicle was parked on your side of the road just round the corner but you could not see beyond it which gear would you need to be prepared to select to make the turn?

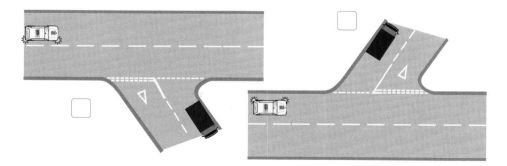

12. When approaching a junction to turn into a side road on a road with an uphill gradient what might you need to do less of but on a down hill gradient more of ?

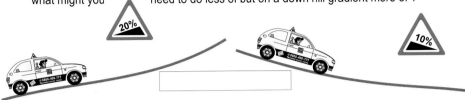

13. In the examples below providing that a clear view into the side road could be obtained would it be permissible to cut the corner or do you believe that under no circumstances should a corner be cut?

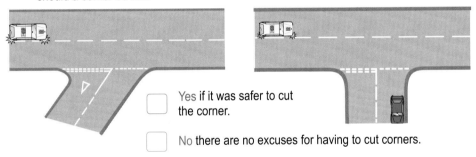

☐ Yes if it was safer to cut the corner.

☐ No there are no excuses for having to cut corners.

14. When you approach an unmarked turning with no lines is it safe to cut the corner?

☐ Yes   ☐ No

15. When turning right from a major road to a side road what road position would you normally adopt prior to turning?

☐ Keep well to the left of the road.

☐ Take up a position in the centre of the road.

☐ Take up a position just left of the centre of the road.

16. The point at which you would need to take up a position just left of the centre of the road when turning right is largely determined by the distance that you need to slow down to negotiate the turning.

True ☐   False ☐

17. The car below is travelling at 30 mph and intends to take the second turning right. Draw two lines to show the path of the front wheels of the car and write each letter of the hazard drill or drills as it would be applied. To help you to do this accurately we have shown the minimum distance in car lengths that you would need to stop at 30 mph (i.e. as if in an emergency).

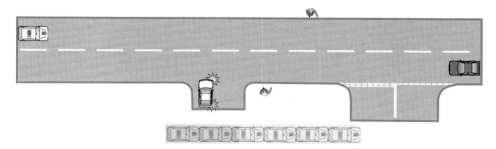

18. By keeping up to date with what is happening behind you can potentially miss out the mirror and signal step if an unpredictable hazard appears which requires an immediate shift of position and/or speed.

True ☐   False ☐

19. The Position step of the hazard drill is considered before adjusting speed to enable following vehicles to pass you as you reduce speed or prevent the need to steer while braking or provide a better view to determine the appropriate speed needed to negotiate the hazard.

True ☐   False ☐

20. When slowing down to turn either right or left from a main road to a side road it would be acceptable to do a block / selective gear change from either 5th or 4th gear to 2nd or even 1st gear.

True ☐   False ☐

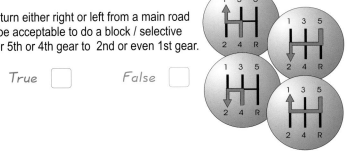

21. If it was necessary to stop before turning into the side roads below please draw a box to show where you would stop.

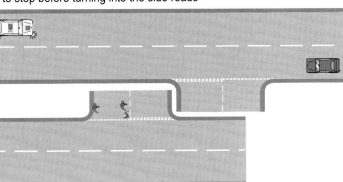

22. Would it be acceptable to stop in fourth gear in the examples shown in the previous question?

Yes ☐   No ☐

23. Would you always need to apply the handbrake and select neutral after stopping to turn left or right?

Yes ☐   No ☐

24. When turning right you look for gaps in the oncoming traffic that would give you time to cross into the side road safely.

Would you need a larger gap if you had to stop first?

Yes ☐   No ☐

25. In the diagram opposite draw an 'X' at the point where you would probably start to turn the steering wheel to turn right. Then draw two lines to show the path of the front wheels of the car as it turned into the side road.

26. What do the following signs tell you is up ahead. Please match the letter denoting the sign to the appropriate description.

A   B   C   D   E

T-Junction.   Side road   Staggered   Junction on   Crossroads.
               to the right.   junction.   bend ahead.

27. In your lesson you may need to emerge out of a side road onto the major road as in the example opposite.

The approach and road position are the same as if you were turning left or right into a side road, however, you will potentially need to stop before turning onto the main road. Please draw two boxes to show where you think you would wait before turning right or left.

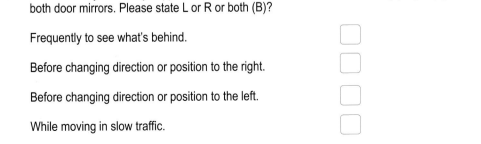

28. When would you usually supplement use of the interior mirror with the left (L), right (R) or both door mirrors. Please state L or R or both (B)?

Frequently to see what's behind.

Before changing direction or position to the right.

Before changing direction or position to the left.

While moving in slow traffic.

29. The car below is turning left and the graph shows the speed of the car as it approaches the turn. Mark an 'X' on the green line at the point where you think the driver finally determined and therefore selected 2nd gear to make this turning.

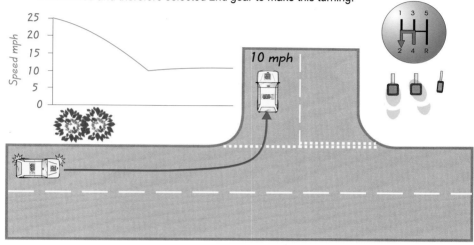

30. This question is the same as the last but this time the gear selected is first gear.

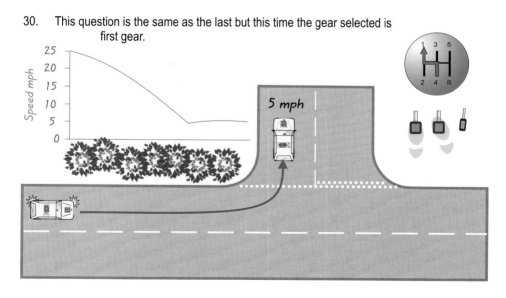

31. This time the driver made two gear changes on approach. Please place the letters A and B at the appropriate points on the green line where you think the gear changes took place. Do you think that two changes were necessary or appropriate?

Yes ☐

No ☐

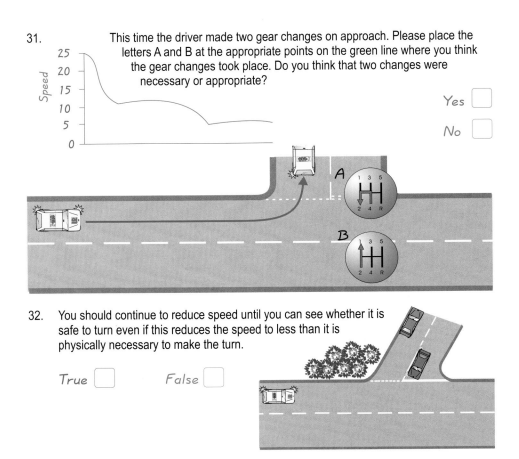

32. You should continue to reduce speed until you can see whether it is safe to turn even if this reduces the speed to less than it is physically necessary to make the turn.

True ☐   False ☐

33. The speed of the vehicle at the point where you can see that it is safe and are physically able to make the turn determines the gear you would block/selectively change to. What gear would you need if the speed at this point was: (Please match the letter denoting the gear change to the appropriate speed).

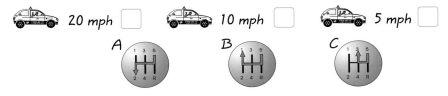

20 mph ☐   10 mph ☐   5 mph ☐

A   B   C

34. In the diagrams below which gear (1st or 2nd) do you think you would probably need to negotiate the turn assuming no moving vehicles are present on the major road?

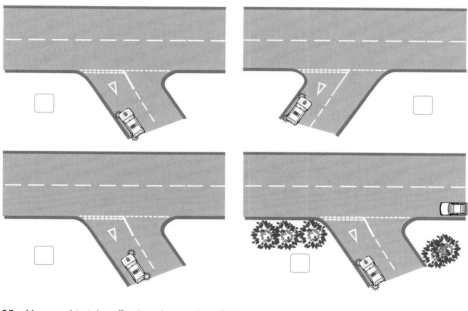

35. You need to take effective observations firstly to the left and then to the right before you emerge.

   True ☐   False ☐

36. When you stop at a give way line it is always necessary to put on the handbrake.

   True ☐   False ☐

37. What is the absolute minimum number of looks you need to make to the left and to the right before you can emerge?

   Number: ☐ Left   ☐ Right

38. Draw the type of lines you would expect to find at the end of the minor roads below, Now draw a box to show where you would position the car if you had to stop or wait.

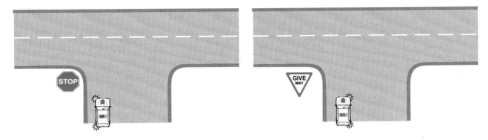

39. In this example which way would you look first to determine whether you would need to wait or not?

Left ☐

Right ☐

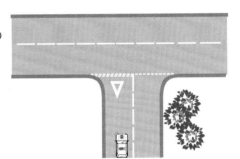

40. Draw two lines to show the path of the front wheels of the car as you emerge to the right (assuming it was clear).

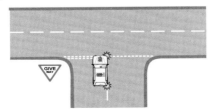

41. Draw two small lines to show where the front wheels of the car would ideally be facing in the examples below:

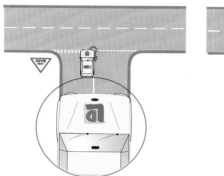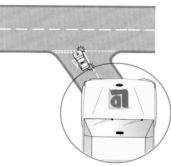

42. At a stop line you must always apply the handbrake.

                True ☐   *False* ☐

43. Once your speed on approach to emerge at a junction drops below 10 mph 1st gear must be selected if you want the option to proceed.

                True ☐   *False* ☐

44. Draw a box to show where you would position the car if you had to stop and wait for traffic on the major road.

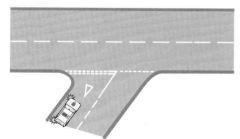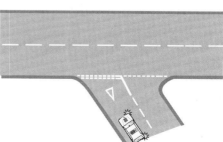

Lesson targets

At the end of the lesson tick those targets below that have been achieved. If any of the targets are ticked as completed with help, review them again after your next lesson.

When I use the hazard drill in general (G) and in particular when turning (T) left (L) or right (R) into side roads or when emerging (E) from them I:

With help from my instructor   *Without help from my instructor*

Identify hazards early and plan my use of the hazard drill.

(1)   (1)

Consider each feature of the drill, even though I may choose not to apply each feature.

(G)(T) (E)   (G)(T) (E)

Supplement use of the interior mirror with my door mirrors as appropriate.

(3)   (3)

Position my vehicle correctly to negotiate the hazard.

(G)(T) (E)   (G)(T) (E)

Adjust my speed so that I don't approach the hazard too quickly or too slowly.

(G)(T) (E)   (G)(T) (E)

Select the best gear for my speed and the hazard I intend to negotiate.

(G)(T) (E)   (G)(T) (E)

Maintain proper observations and act correctly on what I see particularly when crossing traffic as I turn to the right or emerge from a side road.

(TL)(TR) (E)   (TL)(TR) (E)

I use the hazard drill properly to overtake stationary or slow moving vehicles.

(8)   (8)

Lesson 7 - Crossroads

Introduction

Once you can deal with approaching and emerging from basic T-junctions with little support from your instructor the next logical step is to look at crossroads and other more complex junctions. For example junctions with restricted views, acute angles and steep gradients. Again you would be looking to undertake this training in housing estates with minimal traffic at this stage.

Lesson objectives

By the end of this lesson you should be able to:

► recognise crossroads in advance and take extra observations on approach;

► turn left and right from the major road while observing the priority of oncoming traffic;

► emerge left and right from the minor roads, while observing the priorities of traffic on the major road and those on the opposing side road;

► understand the extra observations you need to take at crossroads and the priorities you need to observe;

► recognise when you might use near-side to near-side or off-side to off-side when turning right at a crossroads;

► treat unmarked crossroads as a give way junction while being careful to assess and act upon the actions of other drivers;

► recognise when it is possible to treat a staggered crossroads as two side roads and when it is not;

► deal with more complex junctions that include steep gradients, acute angles and restricted views.

Subject Brief

During this lesson we will learn about how to turn into side roads at crossroads and how to emerge from them.

Approaching crossroads to turn

Approaching to turn into a side road at a crossroads is slightly different from turning into a side road at a T or Y junction. Firstly, traffic may emerge from either side road and cross your path. While you have priority you must be prepared to stop if someone foolishly crosses your path. This may also occur when you intend to go ahead which is why you always take extra observations into the side roads of a crossroads before you pass.

Secondly, when turning right you may be faced with an oncoming vehicle also wanting to turn right. In this instance neither vehicle has priority. Usually vehicles turn nearside to nearside in this situation although offside to offside is safer because you can more easily observe oncoming traffic before turning. Road markings may also dictate which method is used.

Nearside to nearside

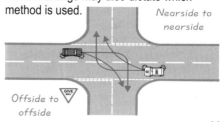

Offside to offside

Emerging at crossroads

If no vehicles are emerging from the side road opposite, emerging to the left and the right is identical to T junctions with the exception that you need to be prepared to take advantage of opportunities to proceed that might arise as a result of the vehicles on the major road slowing down to turn into the side road opposite.

Priorities

Where differences do occur is when vehicles in the opposite side road need to cross your path or follow the same path. Who has priority in these examples is the same as if the two minor side roads were one major road. However do not assume that the other driver will comply.

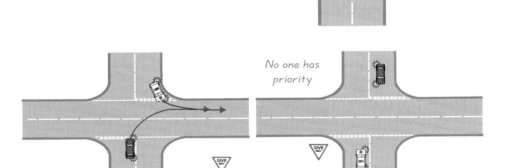

No one has priority

Despite not having priority the other driver may want you to proceed first and therefore you need to learn to watch and anticipate their actions.

In the first example below the green cars progress is blocked by queuing traffic therefore you may proceed despite not having priority because the green car is giving you priority. In the second example it is clear that you can turn without impeding the progress of the green car as the vehicle will need to stop while the driver takes proper observations.

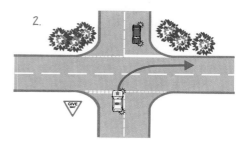

Emerging at staggered crossroads

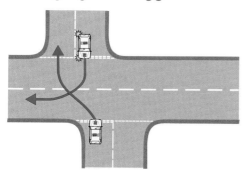

Priorities between the traffic on the opposing side roads is not so clear at staggered crossroads therefore we have to be particularly careful.

Emerging at unmarked crossroads

Neither road is the major road therefore proceed with extreme caution and be prepared to stop. Anticipating other drivers actions and driving at a speed that enables you to stop is critical. Priority regarding oncoming vehicles is not changed.

Lesson quiz

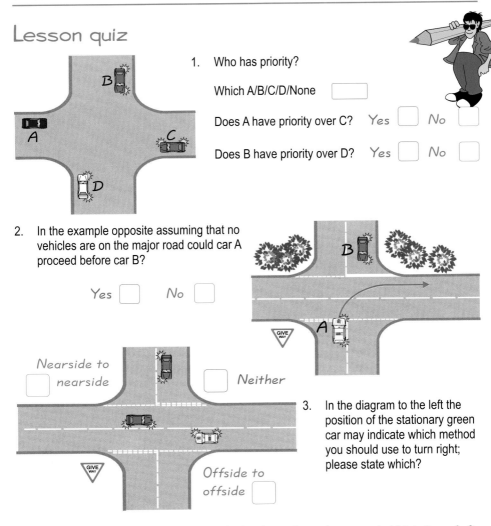

1. Who has priority?

   Which A/B/C/D/None ☐

   Does A have priority over C?   Yes ☐   No ☐

   Does B have priority over D?   Yes ☐   No ☐

2. In the example opposite assuming that no vehicles are on the major road could car A proceed before car B?

   Yes ☐   No ☐

   Nearside to nearside ☐   Neither ☐

   Offside to offside ☐

3. In the diagram to the left the position of the stationary green car may indicate which method you should use to turn right; please state which?

4. Which is the usual method of crossing in the above circumstances and which is the safer?

   Offside to Offside
   Safer ☐
   Usual ☐

   Nearside to Nearside
   Safer ☐
   Usual ☐

5. In the example to the right who has priority?

☐ Car A

☐ Car B

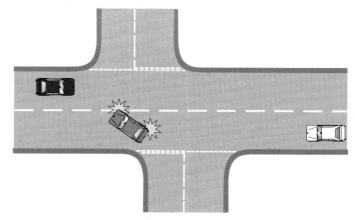

6. In the situation above would the driver of car A really need to watch that car B didn't proceed in front of him or her?

☐ Yes   ☐ No

7. Do you think that this would always be the case?

☐ Yes   ☐ No

8. In the example below was the driver wrong to treat the staggered crossroads as two separate side roads when wanting to cross straight over?

Yes ☐

No ☐

9. In the example below you are going ahead please draw a box to show where you might wait before proceeding.

10. The two cars below both intend to turn right draw two boxes to show where they would potentially wait before turning.

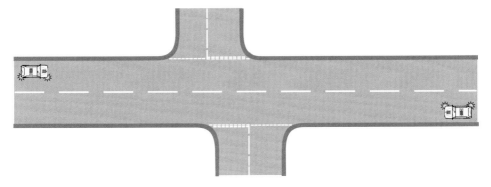

Lesson targets

At the end of the lesson tick those targets below that have been achieved. If any of the targets are ticked as completed with help, review them again after your next lesson.

	With help from my instructor	Without help from my instructor
When on the major road turning right at crossroads I:		
Use nearside to nearside or offside to offside as appropriate.	1	1
When going ahead or turning at crossroads I:		
Always take observations into both side roads.	2	2
When emerging from crossroads, I:		
Always take effective observations before emerging.	3	3
Use nearside to nearside or offside to offside as appropriate.	4	4
Recognize and act upon the priorities but never assume priority.	5	5
When approaching unmarked crossroads, I:		
Treat the junction as a give way.	6	6
Carefully assess and act upon the action of other drivers.	7	7
When emerging at staggered crossroads, I		
Recognize and act upon priorities but am particularly careful not to assume priority.	8	8
Can recognize when it is possible to treat the crossroads as two side roads and when it is not.	9	9

Lesson 8 - Emerging from busier junctions

Introduction

Once you have mastered the routine for approaching and emerging from simpler junctions on quiet roads, with little or no support from your instructor, it's time to move onto dealing with junctions with much more traffic. In particular, you will learn how to cross or join moderately busy traffic streams as you emerge from or enter junctions on roads with varying speed restrictions. This lesson will also be used to further develop your use of the hazard drill as you encounter busier traffic situations.

Lesson objectives

By the end of this lesson you should be able to:

► Explain the importance of timing your approach, assessing gaps in the traffic and having the confidence and ability to move away quickly;

► time your approach to the junction so that you can emerge or cross the path of oncoming traffic safely without the need to stop, where the situation permits;

► position for maximum vision and safety at junctions with restricted sight-lines;

► judge the speed and distance of approaching traffic and determine the size of gap necessary to join or cross traffic streams without impeding the progress of other road users;

► move away briskly from side roads into the major road and from major roads into the side road when a safe opportunity arises.

Subject brief

In this lesson we look at how we emerge from busier junctions.

Emerging at busier junctions

Before you can emerge into a major road with traffic streams you will need to find a gap in the traffic sufficient to build up your speed to theirs either from the left when turning right or from the right when turning left.

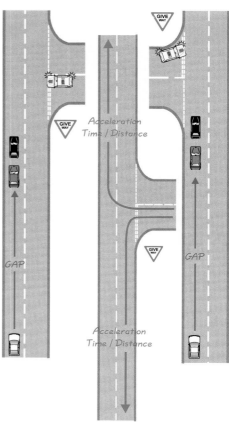

When turning right you will also need a gap to appear in the traffic from the right sufficient to give you time to cross over to the left hand side of the major road. The gap from the right needs to appear at the same time as the gap in the traffic from the left. The gap from the right need not be as long as the one from the left as you are only crossing over to the left side of the road.

If your view of the junction is obscured by parked vehicles continue to creep forward slowly until you can obtain a view as in the example shown.

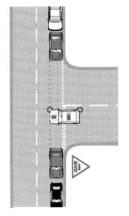

Emerging at Y junctions

The procedure for approaching and emerging from Y junctions is basically the same as T junctions. However, the position of the vehicle may need to be slightly different just prior to emerging to make emerging safer and extra observations must be taken as the pillars of the car may obscure your view and may cause you to miss something small like a motorcycle or pedestrians.

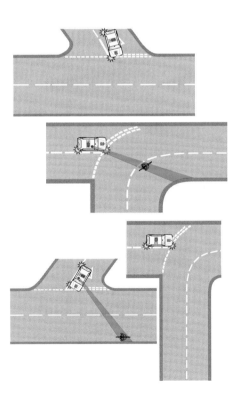

Lesson quiz

1. When emerging to turn right the gap in the traffic;

    ☐ from the right need not be as great
    as that from the left.

    ─── GAP ───▶   ◀─ GAP ─

    ☐ from the left need not be as great
    as that from the right.

    ─ GAP ▶   ◀────── GAP ──

2. Vehicles approaching a junction to emerge have priority over pedestrians
    crossing the mouth of the junction.

    ☐ True   ☐ False

3. In the incident opposite where the vehicle emerging has made a mistake and stopped to let
    you pass what should you do as you
    approach from the right (assuming it is
    safe to proceed)?

    ☐ Give the driver a big smile.

    ☐ Show your disgust using some
    facial or other hand gesture and/or
    blowing the horn.

    ☐ Avoid communicating any feelings
    one way or the other.

71

4. When emerging you may have to select 1st gear having already selected 2nd gear for the turn because either your view of the major road unexpectedly continued to be restricted or a short pause was necessary before proceeding.

    True ☐   False ☐

5. If a short pause at a junction becomes a wait the driver should apply the handbrake and consider selecting neutral.

    True ☐   False ☐

6. If you come across a junction like this and you were going straight ahead please draw a box to show where you might wait before proceeding and two lines to show the path of the front wheels of the car as you negotiate the mini-roundabout.

Do you need to wait to allow the car to turn right?

Yes ☐   No ☐

At a mini-roundabout you give priority to traffic from your left.

☐ True   ☐ False

7. At a mini-roundabout it is not always practical to give a signal as you intend to leave the roundabout:

    True ☐   False ☐

8.   In the incident below you have emerged to turn left and the car approaching from the right gets very close to your rear. You are not sure if you misjudged the speed of the other vehicle or whether the other vehicle had speeded up deliberately to create an incident. You feel embarrassed and put your hand up to apologize. Despite this the other driver flashes the head lights, sounds the horn and is obviously swearing at you. The other driver appears to want you to pull over despite the fact that the vehicles didn't come into physical contact and you did not hear any skidding sound. What should you do?

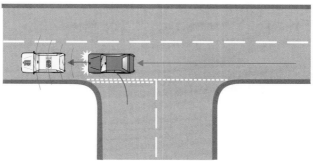

☐   Show your contempt for what you now consider a clear over-reaction by swearing and returning similar hand signals.

☐   Pull up and give the person a piece of your mind.

☐   Pull up and apologize.

☐   Remain calm and try to continue to drive normally and safely.

Lesson targets

At the end of the lesson tick those targets below that have been achieved. If any of the targets are ticked as completed with help, review them again after your next lesson.

When dealing with T or Y junctions, I:

	With help from my instructor	Without help from my instructor
Look out for signs and/or road markings that show the junction type.	①	①
Select the appropriate speed / gear to approach and emerge at open and closed junctions.	O ②C	O ②C
Take the correct course of action at both 'Give-Way' lines and 'Stop' lines.	③	③
Position correctly when approaching and emerging.	T ④Y	T ④Y
Take special care when approaching unmarked junctions.	⑤	⑤
Judge the gap in the traffic needed to emerge safely when turning right and left onto roads of differing speed limits.	30 mph 40 mph ⑥ 50 mph 60 mph	30 mph 40 mph ⑥ 50 mph 60 mph
Keep a special look out for cyclists and motorcyclists.	⑦	⑦
Never assume that I will have priority without first checking for safety.	⑧	⑧
Give priority to pedestrians crossing the mouth of the junction.	⑨	⑨

O = Open junctions, C = Closed junctions, T = T junctions, Y = Y junctions

Lesson 9 - Roundabouts

Introduction

Once you have learnt how to cross and join moderately busy traffic streams from crossroads, T-junctions and Y-junctions it's time to look at dealing with major roundabouts.

Although you may have already dealt with roundabouts in quiet housing estates, in this lesson you will learn how to deal with much more complex roundabouts on major roads with multiple lanes and multiple exits.

Lesson Objectives

By the end of this lesson you should be able to:

- ► Explain the procedure for joining and leaving complex roundabouts with multiple lanes and exits;
- ► recognise roundabouts early and take the necessary observations to ensure you approach the roundabout in the correct lane while looking for opportunities to proceed;
- ► give the appropriate signal on approach for the exit you intend to take;
- ► time your approach speed to make full use of any opportunities to proceed;
- ► identify and respond accordingly to any drivers ahead who may stop unnecessarily at the give way line because they haven't taken the appropriate observations on approach;
- ► exercise good lane discipline throughout the roundabout while anticipating the actions of other drivers and in particular those driving larger vehicles;

- ► correctly apply the hazard drill as you exit the roundabout making sure to signal at the appropriate time and glance to the left as necessary.

Subject brief

Roundabouts are designed to keep the traffic flowing. Traffic should only flow in a clockwise direction around the island in the centre of the roundabout. This circular road is a one-way street and may be made up of one or more lanes. Traffic entering the roundabout must give way to traffic already on the roundabout approaching from the right.

Approaching a roundabout

As with other junctions you apply your hazard drill and take observations of the major road ahead as early as possible. However, unlike other junctions most roundabouts are quite open so that you can assess the flow of traffic on the roundabout at an early stage as you approach the give way lines. The purpose of this is to give you the time to adjust your speed so that, if possible, you can safely emerge into any gaps, in the flow of traffic from the right without stopping.

Unfortunately, some drivers use roundabouts as though they were stop junctions and only take observations to the right at the last minute. As a result they are prone to stopping at the give way line when it isn't necessary.

Therefore, do not assume that the vehicle in front will proceed, even if the way is clear.

How to proceed around a roundabout

Going ahead − − →

Use the left hand lane unless it is a continuation of the dual carriageway or unless signs or road markings show that you should use a different lane. Do not give a signal on approach to the roundabout. Take care to keep in your   lane as you drive around the roundabout.

Turning right · − →

When turning right, approach in the right hand lane and signal right. Maintain your road position and signal left as you pass the exit before the one you need.

Turning left − − →

When turning left, approach in the left hand lane and signal left. Maintain your road position and your signal as you negotiate the roundabout.

Leaving the roundabout

Apply your hazard drill before you exit. Signal your intention to leave the roundabout as you pass the exit before the one that you want to take. If you have to change lanes remember use the interior mirror and left door mirror before you signal and remember to glance to your left before you change lanes to exit.

Lesson quiz

1. Show how you would deal with the roundabout below assuming you wanted to turn right. Firstly, draw a box to show where you would wait if traffic was on the roundabout. Secondly, draw two lines to show the path of the front wheels of the car as you turned to the right.

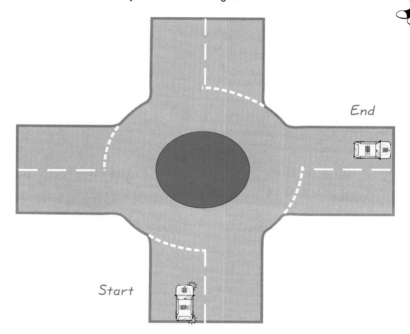

Thirdly, show where you would indicate to the left by placing the letter L on the line you have just drawn. Fourthly, show where you would check your mirrors by writing I interior, O offside (right) and N nearside (left) in the order you would use them.

2. In the example opposite the driver wishes to proceed ahead and can see that the exit road has only one lane. Do you think that any problems would be caused by using the right hand lane on approach to this roundabout?

    Yes ☐   No ☐

    Discuss your answer with your instructor.

3. As you approach the roundabout below you notice a car approaching from the right hand road. Do you think that it would be safe to proceed?

    ☐ Yes   ☐ No

    Discuss your answer with your instructor.

4. The purpose of a roundabout is to keep traffic flowing, this is dependant upon drivers making early observations, particularly to the right and timing their arrival so that they can emerge into a gap in the traffic from the right.

    ☐ True   ☐ False

5. The slower your speed as you approach the roundabout, the bigger the gap you will need in the traffic from the right, to safely emerge.

    True ☐   False ☐

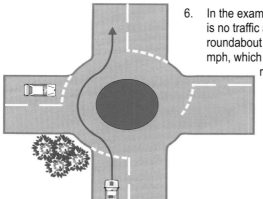

6. In the example to the left, you want to go ahead, there is no traffic approaching from the right, on the roundabout or the side roads. You are travelling at 30 mph, which is slow enough to physically negotiate the roundabout.

    Do you need to slow down?

    Yes ☐   No ☐

Discuss the above answers with your instructor.

7. There are three lanes on the approach to this roundabout. Mark the letters 'L' (=left), 'C' (=centre) and 'R' (=right) in the boxes below to show which lane you would use to approach the roundabout for each exit. Discuss the answer with your instructor.

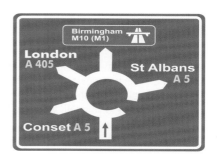

London ☐   Conset ☐

St Albans ☐   Birmingham ☐

8.   Because of the speed that vehicles can sometimes join a roundabout it is vital that you look well down any side roads joining the roundabout from the right for oncoming traffic.

⬜ True   ⬜ False

9.   One of the most common accidents at a roundabout is a rear end collision on approach.

This is usually caused by?

⬜ The driver behind driving too fast on approach.

⬜ The driver in front taking late observations and unexpectedly stopping when he or she could have clearly gone.

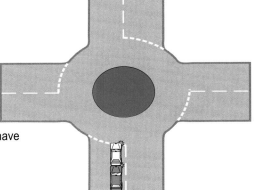

10.   In the diagram opposite draw a line to represent the path you would take if you were taking the fourth exit off the roundabout.

On the diagram place the letter M to show if and when you would check your mirrors and the letter G to show if and when you might glance to your left. Also place the letter S to show when you would signal left to exit the roundabout.

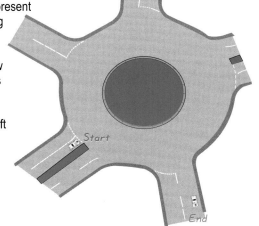

11. Here is a large roundabout with exits labelled A, B, C, D, E. Fill in the table below, to show for each exit:

- Which lane you would use when approaching the roundabout?
- What signal, if any, you would give when approaching the roundabout?
- At which of the numbered points you would signal left to leave the roundabout?

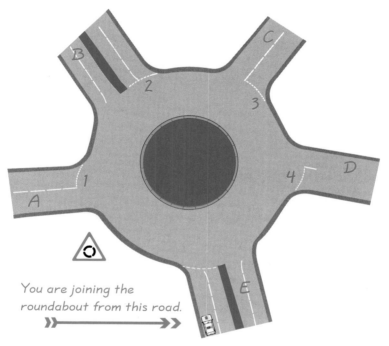

You are joining the roundabout from this road.

EXIT	Approach lane left/right/either	Approach signal left/right/none	Signal to leave at point no. 1/2/3/4
A			
B			
C			
D			
E			

Lesson targets

At the end of the lesson tick those targets below that have been achieved.
If any of the targets are ticked as completed with help, review them again after
your next lesson.

	With help from my instructor	*Without help from my instructor*

When I negotiate a roundabout, I:

Take early observations.

Signal correctly on approach.

Select the correct approach lane for my intended exit.

Control my approach speed to maintain the flow of traffic.

Exercise good lane discipline throughout the roundabout.

Give my exit signal at the correct time,use my mirrors
and if necessary glance to my left.

Take special care if I encounter large vehicles.

Can do all of the above at both large (L) and mini (M)
roundabouts.

Lesson 10 - Pedestrian crossings & traffic signals

Introduction

By now you will have learnt how to deal with all the standard types of junction. Junctions that have larger volumes of traffic where major roads intersect or that are more complex are normally controlled by traffic lights. It's also on these busier major roads that you will come across various types of pedestrian crossings. So the next logical step in your development as a driver is to learn how to deal with traffic light controlled junctions and pedestrian crossings.

Lesson objectives

By the end of this lesson you should be able to:

- ► Explain the traffic light sequence and what each phase means;
- ► explain the similarities and the differences between the various types of pedestrian crossing;
- ► recognise traffic light controlled junctions, pedestrian crossings and school crossing patrols well in advance and apply the hazard drill on approach;
- ► anticipate when traffic lights are likely to change or when pedestrians might cross and be prepared to pull up or move off as necessary;
- ► stop in the correct position at pedestrian crossings being careful never to block the crossing area;
- ► select the correct lane at multiple lane traffic light controlled junctions well in advance and apply a signal as necessary;
- ► act correctly on filter lights at traffic light controlled junctions;

- ► observe priorities when turning right at traffic light controlled crossroads or similar junctions, being careful to position the vehicle in order to turn near-side to near-side or off-side to off-side whichever is appropriate;
- ► recognise when it is inappropriate to proceed even though the lights are in your favour.

Subject brief

During this lesson you will learn about pedestrian crossings, light controlled junctions, traffic signals and crossing patrols.

The pedestrian crossing and traffic signal system

As you drive around you will encounter a range of pedestrian crossings and traffic signals. All of the signals follow the same pattern of meaning.

> RED MEANS STOP BEHIND THE STOP LINE
> AMBER MEANS CAUTION, WARNING OR STOP
> GREEN MEANS THAT YOU MAY PROCEED IF IT IS SAFE

School crossing patrol

The flashing lights on the warning sign inform drivers that a school crossing patrol is ahead. You must give way to the 'lollipop lady' or 'gentleman' on duty and be particularly careful as children will be crossing the road.

Pedestrian crossings

There are several types of pedestrian crossing. In each case you must try to identify the crossing early and properly employ your hazard drill. The zig-zag lines at these crossings act as a warning that there is a pedestrian crossing ahead and mark an area where you must not park or overtake.

You must also be careful not to cross over the studded give way line if you cannot fully clear the crossing area. Apart from the zebra these crossings are light controlled and are push button operated.

Finally, when waiting at a crossing you must never beckon a pedestrian onto a crossing as you may be inviting them into danger.

Zebra

The flashing light on the diagram below is a Belisha Beacon. This marks the location of a zebra crossing, where you see this light you must be prepared to stop and give way to any pedestrians waiting to cross. Once a pedestrian has stepped onto the crossing you must give way and stop.

Pelican

Unlike other pedestrian crossings, Pelican crossings have a flashing amber phase which requires you to give way to pedestrians on the crossing. However, if the crossing is clear you can proceed. At some pelican crossings there is a bleeping sound to indicate to blind or partially-sighted people when the steady green figure is showing. Also note that in the example below, even though there is an island in the middle it is still only one crossing. If it was two crossings it would normally be staggered with a set of lights and a button box on the island.

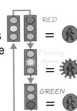

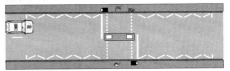

Puffin

Puffin crossings have sensors that determine when the crossing is clear. The signal to change from red, to red/amber, and then to green is automatically triggered at that point. If the pedestrians at the crossing cross the road before getting the green man signal the request to stop traffic is automatically cancelled.

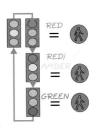

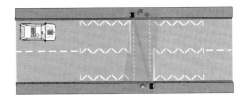

Toucan

Toucan crossings work in exactly the same way as Pelican crossings except that they are also designed to be used by cyclists and there is no flashing amber phase. Cyclists are allowed to ride across these crossings.

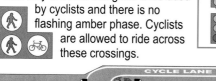

Traffic light crossings

A pedestrian crossing can be incorporated into a normal set of traffic lights. It is still operated by a push button and the crossing area is clearly marked by two rows of studs as shown opposite. When the lights change to green you must watch

carefully for pedestrians still using both crossings before you proceed.

Even though you may have a green light indicating that you can proceed this does not change priorities with regards to oncoming vehicles.

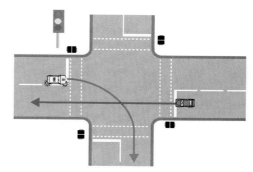

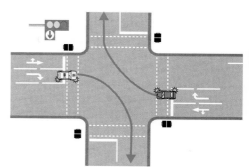

At traffic lights you may find filter lights. Even though the main traffic lights may be red if the filter light is green and pointing in the direction you wish to travel you may proceed.

Traffic signals

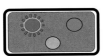

This sign is often used on the approach to traffic lights. If you see it, be prepared for possible traffic queues ahead and be ready to stop. You must always obey the signals, even if the lights are only temporary, for example, at roadworks.

These red lights flash alternately and mean that you must stop to give way to trains or emergency vehicles emerging from their depot. The steady amber light warns you that the red lights are about to show.

If your car breaks down on a railway crossing you must; firstly, get your passengers to safety; secondly, if there is a railway telephone use it to warn the signal operator and thirdly, if possible, push the car off the crossing (however, if the alarm rings or the amber light comes on get well clear of the crossing).

Lesson quiz

1. Enter the letters 'a' to 'e' in the boxes below, to show:

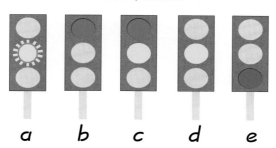

| a | b | c | d | e |

The correct sequence of lights at normal traffic light controlled junctions.

| b | | | | b |

The correct sequence of lights at a pelican crossing.

| b | | | | b |

2. Using the letters 'a' to 'e' (from question 1 above), match the traffic signals in the previous question to the meanings below: (Some meanings may apply to more than one light. If this is the case, enter more than one letter in the box.)

Drive on if safe to do so.

Stop, unless it is dangerous to do so or you have crossed the stop line before the light shows.

You may proceed if the crossing is clear of pedestrians.

Stop and wait.

3. When seen from road 'A', does this traffic signal mean that;

☐ all traffic may proceed?

☐ right turning traffic must wait for a green light?

4. Crossroads at which the traffic lights are out of order should be treated as
.... crossroads.

    (Fill in the missing word.)

5. In the event of a breakdown on a railway level crossing the first priority is to?

☐ Move the car.

☐ Get your passengers clear of the crossing.

☐ Phone the signalman.

KEEP THE
CROSSING
CLEAR

6. As a guide what minimum gap should there be between you and the vehicle in front when stood in a queue of traffic?

☐ Sufficient gap to see the stop lights of the vehicle in front.

☐ Sufficient gap to see the rear tyres of the vehicle in front.

7. You are approaching a queue of traffic just ahead of the pelican crossing. The crossing lights are on green and no pedestrians are near the crossing. Please draw a box to show where you would position your car as you stop.

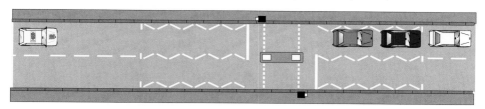

8. When you see someone press a button at a pedestrian crossing will the lights change to red quite quickly if the lights have just changed to green?

☐ Yes   ☐ No

9. You are waiting at this pelican crossing when the flashing amber phase starts. In the example would you normally be allowed to proceed?

Yes ☐

No ☐

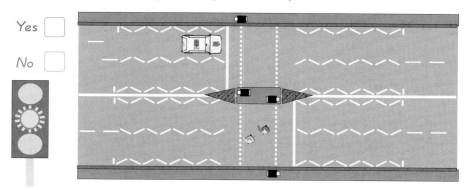

10. When queuing in traffic because you are moving slowly it is not necessary to take frequent looks in the mirrors.

☐ True   ☐ False

11. At the junction opposite what action would you take?

☐ *Stop* ☐ *Proceed*

If you stopped draw a box to show where you would wait.

12. Why would you watch traffic at a set of traffic lights? (Tick two.)

☐ To anticipate when your lights where about to change.

☐ To see if you recognized any of the drivers.

☐ So that you can prepare the car for moving off in advance of the lights changing to green.

Lesson 10 - Pedestrian crossings & traffic signals

Lesson targets

Tick the following items, at the end of your lesson, after discussion with your instructor. All of the targets up to and including this should be completed, without help from your instructor, before moving onto the next part of the course.

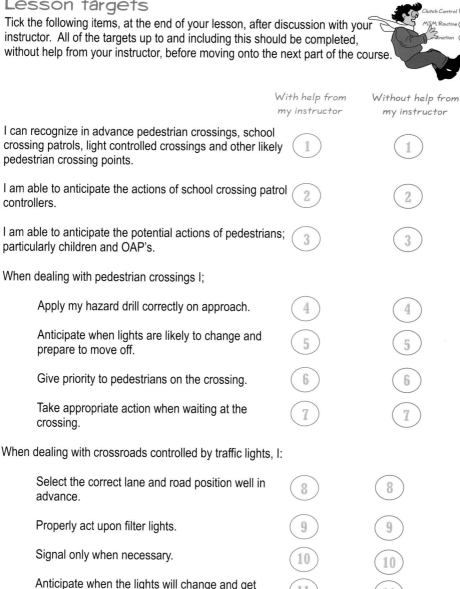

	With help from my instructor	Without help from my instructor
I can recognize in advance pedestrian crossings, school crossing patrols, light controlled crossings and other likely pedestrian crossing points.	1	1
I am able to anticipate the actions of school crossing patrol controllers.	2	2
I am able to anticipate the potential actions of pedestrians; particularly children and OAP's.	3	3

When dealing with pedestrian crossings I;

Apply my hazard drill correctly on approach.	4	4
Anticipate when lights are likely to change and prepare to move off.	5	5
Give priority to pedestrians on the crossing.	6	6
Take appropriate action when waiting at the crossing.	7	7

When dealing with crossroads controlled by traffic lights, I:

Select the correct lane and road position well in advance.	8	8
Properly act upon filter lights.	9	9
Signal only when necessary.	10	10
Anticipate when the lights will change and get ready to move.	11	11

Lesson targets - continued

Recognize and act upon the priorities of oncoming traffic.

12   12

Take up the correct position for turning right.

13   13

Lesson II - Hazard perception & defensive driving

Introduction

By now you should have mastered the main control and procedural skills associated with driving. With these skills in place it's time to move onto part 3 of the Learner Driving programm-traffic skills. To become proficient at handling traffic you will need to further develop your hazard perception and defensive driving skills. Therefore the aim of this lesson is to improve your ability to recognise potential hazards early and to take appropriate defensive action.

Lesson Objectives

By the end of this lesson you should be able to:

- explain the importance of driving proactively rather than reactively;
- explain the difference between an actual hazard and a potential hazard;
- give examples of the kind of clues you are looking for to help you anticipate the types of hazard that may lie ahead;
- look well ahead for signs, other road users, junctions, obstructions and pedestrians;
- assess whether any static road features or the possible actions of other road users represent an actual or potential hazard;
- appropriately apply the hazard drill and plan a suitable course of action to deal with any actual or potential hazard;
- minimise potentially hazardous situations by acting defensively and courteously towards other road users;

- continually adjust speed and position to maintain a safety buffer of space around your vehicle at all times;
- apply the two second rule (or more in adverse weather conditions) and give yourself sufficient room to manoeuvre in traffic queues;
- effectively use signals and the position of your vehicle to communicate your intentions or presence to other road users.

Subject brief

During this lesson you will begin to learn how to deal with much busier traffic situations.

You will recall from Lesson 6 that a hazard may be defined as anything that may require you to change speed, position or direction of your vehicle. Basically hazards can be caused by static road features (e.g. junctions, bends, humps, dips, passing places, traffic lights, bridges, crossings, road works, parked vehicles, wet leaves, spilt oil, ice, snow, surface water etc) or by the actions of other road users or a combination of the two.

Although static road features can present a hazard the routine for dealing with them and the type of hazard they present is covered elsewhere in the Learner Driving programme. In this part of the programme we will be concentrating on those hazards that develop through the actions of other road users and those circumstances that can contribute to their hazardous behaviour.

Hazard Perception; a bit of detection work!

Hazard perception in driving terms can be defined as: 'The art of being able to pick out the important details from all the information provided

by your senses.' A perceptive driver must look for clues and build up a mental picture of what they think may happen next. To anticipate the actions of other road users and to determine any risks.

While hazard perception skills can only truly be acquired through experience (preferably under the guidance of an appropriately qualified driving instructor) you can speed up the learning process by having a better understanding of the factors that an expert driver considers when building up this mental picture of what's likely to happen next. These are the factors that an expert driver would consider:

Road Signs

Road signs can provide you with a clear warning of what lies ahead. It is essential that you train yourself to take note of all road signs and act accordingly.

Your Location

Are you in a busy town centre or on a country road? It would be unlikely that you would meet a flock of sheep in the High Street, but there may be one just around the next corner on a country road. Whatever your location you must always consider the type of hazard that you may expect to meet

there, and be driving at such a speed that you can stop safely, if necessary.

The Time of Day

The time of day can give you a lot of information about what to expect on the road. If you see a warning sign for cattle, or mud on the road you should be especially vigilant at dawn or dusk because cows are often taken for milking at these times and may well be on the road ahead ... perhaps around the next bend.

Although children can be present in the road at any time, they are out in force just before and after school. Therefore, you should be keeping a special look out for children during the morning rush hour and mid-afternoon periods.

Other Road Users

It may seem fairly obvious that you should look out for other road users, but remember, you are not just looking for them, you are looking for clues about what they will do next?

Pedestrians: The Highway Code explains that those pedestrians most at risk on the road are over 60 and less than 15. Old people do not judge speed and distance very well and their reactions can be slow. Have they seen you? Can they hear you? Look for clues. Are they carrying a white stick? Are they looking your way? And so on.

Children have little time to consider road safety; they are more interested in the game that they are playing or the ice cream van that they are running after. Look for clues. Are they alone? If one child runs or cycles into the road there will often be at least one more following; footballs are followed by children; cycles, seemingly abandoned at the side of the road, will mean that children are not far away.

All pedestrians, not just the young and old, are at risk on the road. If there are pedestrians about, make sure that you know what they are going to do before they do it.

Animals: Noise and vehicles frighten animals. Therefore, drive slowly, don't sound your horn or rev up the engine and keep your distance. Watch their behavior carefully, particularly if it is a horse being ridden by a child.

Cyclists: A High Court judge once ruled that a cyclist is entitled to wobble. Drivers should have more control over their vehicles than cyclists who are dependent upon physical strength and effort to pilot their machines. Always leave plenty of room when passing cyclists, look out for clues about their next move. For example, a cyclist who looks around over his or her right shoulder may be about to turn right; a puddle in the road will cause a cyclist to move out. Cyclists are not easy to see and they can easily get lost in the blind spots around your vehicle. Particularly watch out for them in slow moving traffic in built up areas - they may overtake you on either side when you least expect.

Motorcyclists: Like cyclists motorcyclists are not easy to see particularly at dusk and at night. Like cyclists they may also take up unusual road positions to avoid holes and bumps in the road surface. It is very easy to miss an approaching motorcyclist when emerging at junctions so remember think once, think twice, think bike!

Drivers: If you are unsure about what a driver is going to do next, leave plenty of space between you and them. A sporty looking "custom-car" may be driven by someone more interested in "posing" than driving. Look out for the actions of drivers: a driver who has just stopped may open his door without checking to see if it is safe; a driver who seems to be dithering about may be a stranger to the area and could, therefore, make a last minute turn without a signal when he sees the road that he is looking for.

Large vehicles: Buses and large vehicles need more room and may take up unusual road positions to turn round corners at junctions etc. Hold back and give them plenty of room.

Inconsistent behaviour

Inconsistent behaviour is often a very good clue to what might happen next. Just because a bus is signalling left prior to the side road that you intend to emerge from doesn't mean that you should go on the assumption that the bus is turning left? Look to see if all the actions of the driver are consistent with the signal. Is the vehicle slowing down as you would expect to complete the proposed turn? Is the position of the vehicle consistent with the proposed manoeuvre? Is the driver looking in the direction they intend to turn? Could the driver be signalling left for any other reason? In this example the bus driver may be signalling left to pull up at a bus stop just after the side road. Make sure you look at all the evidence before you finally decide.

Lets consider another example. If you were driving behind a vehicle that was indicating to turn left but the road on the left had a no entry sign at its entrance it is quite probable that the driver will do an emergency stop or swerve away at the last minute once he or she realises the mistake. Therefore anything that would potentially prevent the driver from completing the proposed manoeuvre safely would make the proposed action inconsistent.

Train your mind to recognise inconsistency - that's not quite right why's that?

What other drivers cannot see

Consider what you can see that other drivers cannot see. This may play an important part in determining what may happen next. As well as determining whether the drivers behaviour is consistent with the manoeuvre they propose to complete also consider whether you can see something or someone that they cannot see that may cause them to alter their course or abort the manoeuvre at the last minute. Also consider whether other drivers need to see you and if so determine what you can do to make your presence know to them.

The weather and visibility

Bright sunlight, fog, rain and snow can severely affect visibility therefore remember to slow down and give yourself more space. At dusk and at night the driver loses the ability to see any detail and dark objects easily merge into the background. Consider not only how this may affect your judgement but also how these conditions may affect other drivers. Is the other driver being blinded by bright sunlight or if at night by headlights on full beam? Are the windows of other vehicles misty - can the driver see you? Will the high-sided vehicle, in high wind, remain stable when it crosses a gap in the hedge or buildings that might line the side of the road? Also remember the effects of water, ice and snow on the road surface - are the other drivers driving too fast for the weather conditions - are you driving too fast for these conditions?

Defensive driving

Driving defensively is all about giving you time to react and keeping your options open. Even someone with lightening  fast reactions needs time to react. The laws of physics simply prevent a car from stopping dead. Even if you are Superman or Superwoman, with supernatural reactions, you couldn't stop a car within fewer car lengths than those shown opposite:

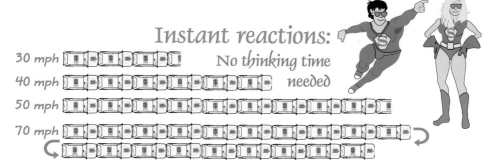

Consequently, anything or anybody who is within the above distances of the front of your car will be hit! You could call this area to the front of your car the impact zone or if you are travelling at 40 MPH or more the killing zone as anyone hit at these speeds is unlikely to survive. This clearly demonstrates the importance of anticipating what might happen and acting upon that rather than waiting until it happens. To do this effectively you need to:

- Look well ahead and perceive potential problems early.

- Apply your hazard drill in good time.

- Give yourself plenty of space.

Look well ahead and perceive potential problems early

See and be seen. Take up safe road positions that allow you to see and be seen. Be attentive; focus on the driving task - don't let your mind wander. Keep your eyes moving and scan the road well ahead. Avoid staring at any single point ahead or to the side. Concentrate on the available space (i.e. the gaps), not the obstructions.

With experience and guidance from your instructor you will begin to recognise what feedback from your senses is important and what is not. Ignore the superficial information you can see. For example don't concentrate on identifying individual drivers or pedestrians or the make, model or the colours of vehicles. Instead concentrate on the position, speed and potential course of other vehicles and/or pedestrians both to the front, rear and sides of your vehicle.

Look as far down the road as you can see for any potential hazards whether they are static road features or situations being caused by other road users. A gap in the tree line ahead may mean that there is a side road at that point or an upside down triangle sign in the distance may warn you that you are approaching a T Junction and so on.

Initially you may perceive risks that aren't really there or indeed ignore risks that are. With experience you will begin to develop your own judgement in this regard.

Apply the hazard drill in good time

As soon as you perceive a potential danger begin to employ the hazard drill and determine where you can go or how you can stop if the danger materializes. Remember you need to consider what's behind as well as what is in front when considering your options. The hazard drill was covered in some detail earlier in the programme in lesson 6.

Give yourself plenty of space - driving in space

You need to give yourself the time to recognise a potential problem and apply the hazard drill. We refer to this as "driving in space". Driving in space is all about maintaining a buffer of 'safety space' or if you like a bubble all around you at all times. The higher your speed (or greater your stopping distance) the bigger the bubble needs to be.

● Space to the front

Always allow yourself enough room to stop. On narrow country roads with a limited view, this may be as much as twice your overall stopping distance (to leave room for the idiot coming the other way!).

● Space to the sides

Make sure that you leave enough room for pedestrians, cyclists, motorcyclists and other vehicles. If you are unsure whether or not you will fit through a gap, you won't! Give parked cars and pedestrians at the side of the road plenty of clearance. Remember pedestrians are far more vulnerable then vehicles. Allow for car doors opening or children appearing from between parked cars or pedestrians wandering onto the road particularly in crowded streets. Position your car accordingly and reduce speed as the space to your sides is reduced.

● Space to the rear

If other vehicles follow too close slow down and let them pass. Remember that it's your neck that will suffer if someone hits your car from the back! The less space you have at the back the more you need at the front.

ONLY A FOOL BREAKS THE TWO-SECOND RULE

KEEP A MINIMUM SAFETY GAP OF TWO SECONDS

Lesson quiz

1. To help you appreciate how much distance you cover in relation to time please complete the table below. See speed and distances in Lesson 5, page 38.

Speed	Distance covered per second	Approximate car lengths per second
30 MPH	metres	
40 MPH	metres	
50 MPH	metres	
60 MPH	metres	

2. You wish to pull up just after the junction on the left. What signal should you give?

☐ Give just a short signal to the left to let the driver ahead know you do not mean to turn left.

☐ Be courteous and flash your headlights to tell the car ahead that you are about to pull up and he can go.

☐ Press your brake pedal to let vehicles behind know you are slowing down and use the slowing down hand signal (optional).

3. Some blind people carry a white stick. Tick one answer, below, to indicate the impaired abilities of someone who is carrying a white stick with two red reflective bands.

    ☐ Deaf and dumb

    ☐ Blind and deaf

    ☐ Deaf

4. If the driver in the car behind you wants to break the speed limit, you should:

    ☐ Allow the car to overtake you.

    ☐ Prevent the car from overtaking because speeding is illegal.

    ☐ Drive faster to keep out of the way.

5. In the diagram below, The green car, 'C', is parked. The driver of car 'A' is flashing the headlamps. Tick one of the statements below to explain what you would do if you were driving car 'B'.

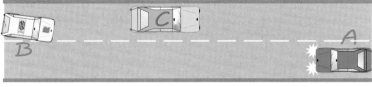

    ☐ Assume that it is safe to pass the green car.

    ☐ Give way to driver 'A' whatever happens.

    ☐ Watch the actions of driver 'A' before deciding what to do.

6. Arm signals can sometimes be used to reinforce flashing indicator signals.

    True ☐   False ☐

7. Other drivers may sometimes give incorrect signals. Using good observation you can often identify when this is the case.

    Here is a list of possible 'clues' which might lead you to realize that a signal is being used incorrectly. Tick those which you think are genuine clues to show that the driver might not intend to do the manoeuvre that the signal suggests.

    ☐   The driver's speed is too fast for the manoeuvre.

    ☐   The car is in the wrong position for the proposed manoeuvre.

    ☐   The driver is not looking in the direction of travel.

    ☐   An arm signal has been given instead of an indicator signal.

    ☐   There is more than one possible manoeuvre associated with the signal.

    ☐   There is an obstruction preventing the proposed manoeuvre.

8. Draw two boxes, on the diagram below, to show where you would position your car, if you were travelling behind the red car at the same speed and leaving the minimum safe separation gap.

    a: On a dry road.   b: On a wet road.

    | 6 | 5 | 4 | 3 | 2 | 1 |

    The above numbers represent the number of seconds you would be behind the red car at this speed.

9. The Highway Code gives advice about driving in fog. Tick 'True' or 'False' for each statement below, to show how you would drive in foggy conditions.

	True	False
You should only use fog lights if visibility is seriously reduced.	☐	☐
You should allow extra time for journeys in fog.	☐	☐
You should try and follow the tail lights of the vehicle in front.	☐	☐
If you can see the vehicle in front in thick fog you are probably following too closely.	☐	☐
If the car behind is following too close in fog, it is a good idea to accelerate, in order to get away from it.	☐	☐
It is a good idea to use your brake lights whenever you slow down in fog as this acts as a warning for following drivers.	☐	☐
If roadside signals show the word 'fog', when weather seems to be clear, you should ignore it as they are probably showing by mistake.	☐	☐
You should be aware of your speed in fog. You may be travelling faster than you think.	☐	☐
You should try to avoid use of windscreen wipers in foggy conditions.	☐	☐

10. You are waiting to turn right and the oncoming green car stops as it approaches a queue of traffic and the driver flashes the headlights. What should you do?

☐ Wait as the flashing headlight signal is not a recognized signal.

☐ Proceed to turn right while being particularly careful to watch for any cyclists or motorcyclists coming up the sides of the vehicle that has given way to you.

11. In the example below you unexpectedly find a stationary queue of traffic around the bend what signal should you consider using once you have stopped?

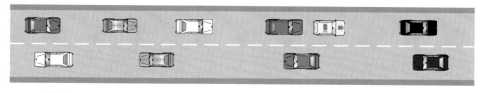

12. You are travelling at 30 mph and the vehicle behind is tailgating (i.e. too close) what should you do?

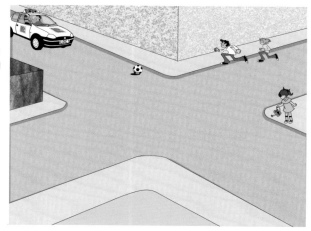

☐ Increase your speed to create a gap.

☐ Slow down to increase the gap in front.

☐ Pull up on the left and let the driver behind pass.

13. There are several potential dangers in the situation shown in the picture. As the driver of the car what do you think they are?

Circle the potential dangers.

14. What hazard might you reasonably expect to encounter after this road sign? (Tick one answer.)

☐ High vehicles in the centre of the road.

☐ Overhead cables.

☐ Hump-back bridge.

15. In the example opposite the car approaching from the right appears to be travelling a little too fast to turn left what should you do?

Proceed ☐   Wait ☐

Lesson targets

At the end of the lesson tick those targets below that have been achieved. If any of the targets are ticked as completed with help, review them again after your next lesson.

Visual scanning

With help from my instructor   *Without help from my instructor*

When driving I always:

Keep my eyes moving and scan the road ahead.   (1)   (1)

Avoid staring at any single point ahead or to the sides.   (2)   (2)

Concentrate on the available space, not the obstructions.   (3)   (3)

Perception

When driving I:

Anticipate the actions of other road users.   (4)   (4)

Spot and act upon road signs.   (5)   (5)

Spot and act upon junctions and other physical features or hazards.   (6)   (6)

Defensive driving strategy

I have practiced the following defensive driving strategies.

Showing courtesy towards other drivers.   (7)   (7)

Followed other vehicles using the two-second-rule.   (8)   (8)

Allowed another driver to overtake.   (9)   (9)

Held back to give way to approaching traffic when I have been unsure about going through a narrow gap.   (10)   (10)

Lesson targets (continued)

	With help from my instructor	Without help from my instructor
Acted correctly when another driver has flashed his/her headlights.		
Used my horn correctly to warn another road user of my presence.		
In addition to all of the above, I know how to drive defensively in adverse weather conditions.		

Lesson 12 - Dual Carriageways

Introduction

Once you have improved your hazard perception and defensive driving skills you are ready to face the challenge of dealing with fast moving traffic on dual carriageways. Therefore the aim of this lesson is to learn how to deal with slip roads, overtaking and the extra hazards caused by fast moving traffic on dual carriageways. The key to dealing with this traffic is good forward observations to assess the traffic situation ahead and the effective use of mirrors to assess the traffic situation behind.

Lesson objectives

By the end of this lesson you should be able to:

► join a dual carriageway from a slip road by building up speed to match that of the traffic on the dual carriageway;

► leave a dual carriageway safely by using the slip road, not the carriageway, for decelerating;

► cross or turn right from a dual carriageway safely, paying particular attention to the extra problems this causes;

► exercise good lane discipline and use of the two-second rule;

► maintain good progress and overtake other vehicles as necessary;

► anticipate the actions of other drivers and apply the hazard drill appropriately;

► demonstrate a good awareness of what's happening behind.

Subject brief

During this lesson you will learn about dual carriageways. The term dual carriageway simply refers to a road where there is a physical separation between streams of traffic travelling in opposite directions. The barrier is usually a grass verge in the centre of the road (with or without a crash barrier).

Each side of the dual carriageway can have a number of lanes (typically two or three). Keep to the left-hand lane unless signs or road markings indicate otherwise or unless you are overtaking.

Dual carriageway ahead

End of dual carriageway

Watch out for the 'end of dual-carrigeway' sign. Don't start to overtake after you see the sign, otherwise you might run out of road or even worse, find yourself facing an oncoming vehicle head on!

Clearways

Clearways are not restricted to dual-carriageways. However, most dual carriageways are clearways. On roads with the clearway sign you must not stop on the main carriageway except at a layby. Clearways are designed to allow the free flow of traffic.

Junctions and slip roads

All the usual junction types can be found on dual carriageways (including traffic light controlled). On dual carriageways cars are allowed to travel at speeds up to 70 mph so you can imagine the difficulty in judging potential gaps in the traffic that you need when emerging from a junction to turn right or left onto a dual carriageway or when you cross a carriageway to turn right. To help reduce the dangers slip roads were developed. A slip road is the term commonly used to describe an acceleration or deceleration lane that helps to maintain the flow of traffic on the dual carriageway by providing a much safer way to join and leave fast flowing traffic. It is the only method allowed on motorways.

Using slip roads

A slip road can be used to build up your speed such that you can time your entry on to the carriageway to coincide with a suitable gap in the traffic from your right. The objective is to match the speed of the traffic on the carriageway such that the gap needed will be minimal.

If you are travelling at a slower speed then the gap needed will have to be much larger. Unfortunately slip roads come in varying lengths therefore it is not always possible to match the speed of the traffic you intend to merge with. Consequently, even before you commence the manoeuvre of joining a carriageway you must assess the length of the slip road to determine what speed you can attain and what gaps there are in the traffic from your right. Once you can see a reasonably sized gap coming towards you in the mirrors adjust your speed such that you can reach the speed you need to merge safely at the same time as the

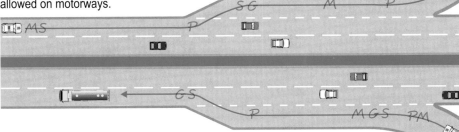

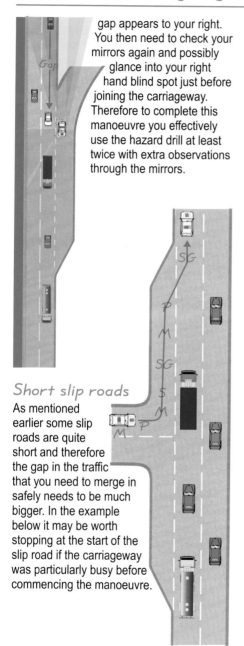

gap appears to your right. You then need to check your mirrors again and possibly glance into your right hand blind spot just before joining the carriageway. Therefore to complete this manoeuvre you effectively use the hazard drill at least twice with extra observations through the mirrors.

Short slip roads

As mentioned earlier some slip roads are quite short and therefore the gap in the traffic that you need to merge in safely needs to be much bigger. In the example below it may be worth stopping at the start of the slip road if the carriageway was particularly busy before commencing the manoeuvre.

If possible, when a slip road is available to leave a dual carriageway you should try to avoid reducing your speed until you have entered the slip road. If the slip road is too short to allow you to do this then you would need to reduce speed before you entered the slip road. In which case you effectively use your hazard drill twice, once to reduce speed just prior to entering the slip road and once just as you begin to enter the slip road.

Overtaking

When you overtake on a dual carriageway you would use your hazard drill at least three times. Once to get ready to overtake, once to actually overtake and once to move back into the left hand lane.

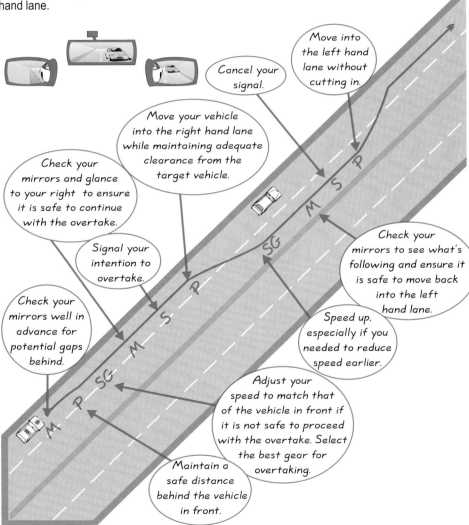

Move into the left hand lane without cutting in.

Cancel your signal.

Move your vehicle into the right hand lane while maintaining adequate clearance from the target vehicle.

Check your mirrors and glance to your right to ensure it is safe to continue with the overtake.

Signal your intention to overtake.

Check your mirrors to see what's following and ensure it is safe to move back into the left hand lane.

Check your mirrors well in advance for potential gaps behind.

Speed up, especially if you needed to reduce speed earlier.

Adjust your speed to match that of the vehicle in front if it is not safe to proceed with the overtake. Select the best gear for overtaking.

Maintain a safe distance behind the vehicle in front.

Lesson quiz

1. Label the signs to show their meanings by writing 'a', 'b' or 'c' in the appropriate box.

a: Traffic merging from the left.

b: Traffic merging from the right.

c: 'T' junction ahead.

2. When turning right, onto or off a dual carriageway, you cross a gap in the middle of the carriageway:

You may not stop in this gap.	True ☐	False ☐
You should always stop in this gap.	True ☐	False ☐
You may stop in this gap to give way to oncoming traffic.	True ☐	False ☐
You may stop in this gap if it is big enough to accommodate your car without it protruding onto either carriageway.	True ☐	False ☐

3. Apply the hazard drill, to the following right turn off a dual carriageway, by placing the letters M,S,P,S,G on the car's path.

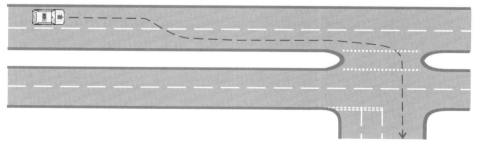

4. Do the same again for this left turn off a dual carriageway.

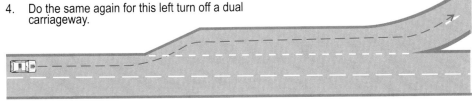

5. The signs shown below are countdown markers. They are placed 100 yards apart on the approach to:

a: The start of a dual carriageway.

b: An exit from a dual carriageway.

c: The start of a motorway.

Write 'a', 'b' or 'c' in the box

6. You have just started to overtake a long line of traffic in the left hand lane of a dual carriageway. When should you cancel your signal?

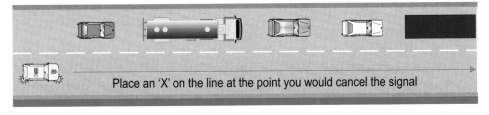

Place an 'X' on the line at the point you would cancel the signal

7. Under no circumstance should you overtake on the left hand lanes of a dual carriageway.

True ☐   False ☐

8. When driving in lanes on a dual carriageway where would you normally position your vehicle:

To the left of the lane.

To the right of the lane.

To the centre of the lane.

9. The central and right hand lane of a three lane dual carriageway would usually be for:

1. Overtaking.
2. To separate faster moving traffic from slower moving traffic.
3. To separate traffic that is going ahead or turning right.

Which 1 / 2 / 3 ?

Which of the other alternatives might be appropriate depending on the road marking on approach to a junction?

10. You should try to avoid driving in the blind spots of any vehicles ahead of you.

 True

 False

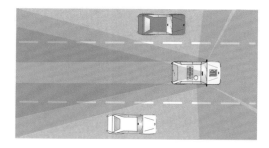

11. Up ahead you can see that a vehicle is about to merge from the left. What should you do?

☐ Maintain your current course and speed.

☐ Move into the right hand lane if it is safe to do so.

☐ Slowdown or speed up to help the other driver.

12 You notice a lorry begins to signal right just as you were about to overtake it. What should you do?

☐ Speed up to get past the lorry quickly.

☐ Begin to signal right to warn the lorry driver that you are going to overtake him or her.

☐ Apply your hazard drill and be prepared to slow down to allow the lorry to move over into the right hand lane.

13. In the last situation (question 12) what might give you a clue that the lorry driver intends to go (G) or wait (W). Write (G) or (W) below:

☐ The brake lights come on.

☐ The lorry's speed increases.

☐ The position of the lorry moves slightly to the right.

☐ The vehicle in front of the lorry is moving very slowly.

☐ The lorry driver cancels the signal.

14. You are on a 3 lane dual carriageway overtaking vehicles at a speed of 70 mph, when a car, clearly exceeding the speed limit, appears behind with the headlights flashing. What should you do?

☐ Immediately brake hard and pull in behind the car just to your left after checking your mirrors.

☐ Increase your speed to that of the car behind you.

☐ Overtake the car just to your left and then immediately pull into the central lane.

☐ Continue until you can see a better gap in the traffic to your left and then move over to let the car behind pass.

15. You are approaching a slip road to merge into the traffic on a dual carriageway when you can see that there are no suitable gaps in the traffic from your right for you to safely merge in, what should you do?

Which 1/2/3/4 ?

1. Wait until you can see gaps approaching before going onto the slip road.

2. Proceed onto the slip road and commence accelerating in the hope that someone will let you in; but being prepared to stop at the end of the slip road if nobody does.

3. As 2 but continue onto the hard shoulder rather than stopping at the end of the slip road.

4. Proceed onto the slip road driving slowly while waiting for a gap to appear and then accelerate.

16. This is the same as the last question but this time you cannot see the approaching traffic from the right until you are on the slip road. Therefore only options 2, 3 and 4 are applicable.

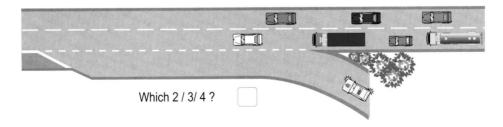

Which 2 / 3/ 4 ?

17. You are driving along and you see someone trying to join the dual carriageway
from the left. What should you do?

☐ Slow down to give the driver space to emerge in front of you or
speed up to allow the driver to merge behind you before they
reach the end of the slip road.

☐ Move to the right lane.

☐ Just maintain your current speed and allow the other driver
to decide when to merge.

18. The driver below could mistake the Y junction for a _____ which could be quite
dangerous.

19. In the example below draw two lines to show the path of the front wheels of the car as you would turn right onto this dual carriageway. Also draw a box to show where you might position the car in the middle if you feel it would be appropriate to stop halfway and do the manoeuvre in two steps.

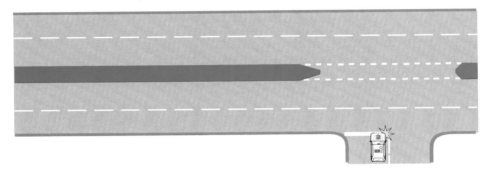

20. This diagram shows one side of a dual carriageway. Write the speed limits for each section of the road in the boxes provided. Also state whether it is a minimum (min) or maximum (max) limit.

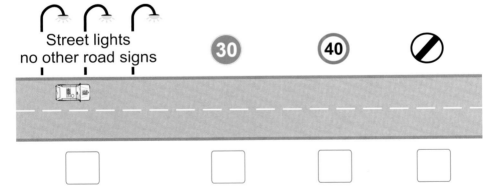

Lesson targets

At the end of the lesson tick those targets below that have been achieved. If any of the targets are ticked as completed with help, review them again after your next lesson.

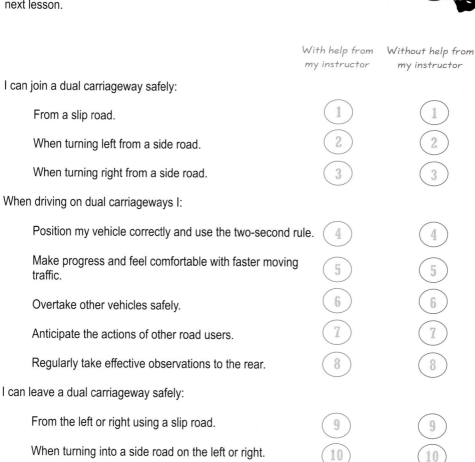

	With help from my instructor	Without help from my instructor
I can join a dual carriageway safely:		
From a slip road.	1	1
When turning left from a side road.	2	2
When turning right from a side road.	3	3
When driving on dual carriageways I:		
Position my vehicle correctly and use the two-second rule.	4	4
Make progress and feel comfortable with faster moving traffic.	5	5
Overtake other vehicles safely.	6	6
Anticipate the actions of other road users.	7	7
Regularly take effective observations to the rear.	8	8
I can leave a dual carriageway safely:		
From the left or right using a slip road.	9	9
When turning into a side road on the left or right.	10	10

Introduction

The experience you have gained so far will prove invaluable as you take the next step in the programme, which is to move into busy town and city centres. Therefore the aim of this lesson is to learn how to deal with the road systems and the traffic conditions found in busy town and city centres.

Lesson objectives

By the end of this lesson you should be able to:

► Identify the types of hazard that are likely to occur in busy town or city centres;

► recognise when you are entering or crossing a one-way street;

► maintain all around awareness when in traffic queues or on multiple lane roads;

► show courtesy to other road users and avoid blocking side roads or crossing traffic at junctions;

► plan well ahead and select the correct lane as soon as possible for the route you intend to take;

► merge with or join queuing traffic streams from side roads or other lanes;

► recognise cycle, bus and tram lanes and act accordingly;

► recognise parking and traffic flow restrictions.

Subject brief

During this lesson you will learn how to deal with other road users in busy town and city centres. You will be encountering one way traffic systems; bus, cycle and possibly tram lanes; and various parking restrictions.

Traffic queues

In town and city centres you often find traffic queuing. Therefore don't expect the road ahead to be clear. Traffic queues can sometimes make it difficult to get into the correct lane. Therefore you should always try to get into your designated lane as early as possible. However, even with the best planning there may be times when you might signal to change lanes and rely upon the courtesy of another driver to allow you to merge in front of them. In this instance the signal becomes a request to merge rather than a signal that you intend to immediately change lanes. However, you must continue to allow traffic to flow in your current lane and be prepared to abandon your manoeuvre if no one lets you in.

If someone signals to merge in front of you make sure they have seen you and that their actions are consistent with a request to merge rather than an intention to immediately move across. Then if it is safe to give them priority do so. Courtesy and common sense plays a very important role in town and city centre driving.

While queuing you have to particularly watch for pedestrians coming onto the road in front of you and for cyclists or motorcyclists coming up either side of your vehicle. All round observations and awareness are critical when in queues of traffic.

One way systems

To help improve the flow of traffic around town and city centres one

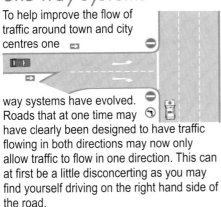

way systems have evolved. Roads that at one time may have clearly been designed to have traffic flowing in both directions may now only allow traffic to flow in one direction. This can at first be a little disconcerting as you may find yourself driving on the right hand side of the road.

Although you will be familiar with driving in the right hand lane on a dual carriageway the right hand lanes in a one way system are not specifically for overtaking. On a one way system traffic may overtake on either side. Also traffic can equally merge from the right as well as from the left. On dual carriageways traffic usually only merges from the left.

Bus, cycle and tram lanes.

Many town and city centres now specially cater for buses and cyclists by providing specific lanes for such traffic. Some also cater for trams.

Cycle lanes are protected by a solid white line that should not be crossed. Special care must be taken if you cross a cycle lane when turning left or right. Areas of the road may also be designated for cyclists.

Watch out for road markings like those above. Note how space is allocated in front of the traffic for cyclists at the set of traffic lights. You would be required to stop behind the second white line before the traffic lights not the first.

Bus lanes may or may not be for the exclusive use of buses. If there are only certain times when buses have exclusive use of such lanes road signs will clearly state this. Outside of these times normal traffic may use them.

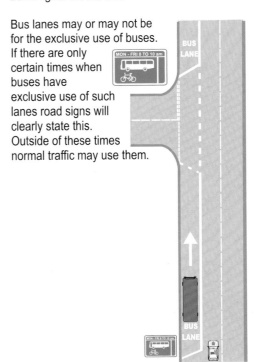

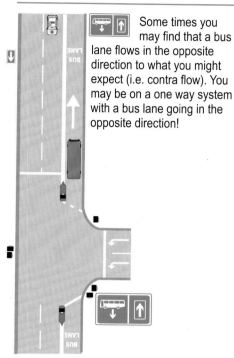

Some times you may find that a bus lane flows in the opposite direction to what you might expect (i.e. contra flow). You may be on a one way system with a bus lane going in the opposite direction!

In an attempt to reduce the traffic congestion of city centres some councils have adopted modern tram systems. You should always be prepared to give way to trams as they cannot stop easily and cannot be steered. The metal tracks or rails also present a hazard as they provide little road adhesion and can be very slippy particularly when wet.

Parking restrictions

Parking restrictions are designated by signs and yellow lines. Different types of yellow line indicate the various levels of restriction in force.

A simple rule to remember is - the more paint there is the greater the restriction. Always look out for the yellow or blue plates that give details of the limitations on parking.

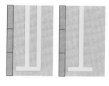

Parking restrictions in force

Details of the parking restriction

Lesson quiz

1. This diagram shows a one-way street divided into three lanes. Mark 'a', 'b' or 'c', in the box, to show where you should position your vehicle when driving in the right-hand lane.

   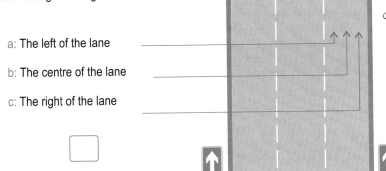

   a: The left of the lane

   b: The centre of the lane

   c: The right of the lane

2. The learner shown in this diagram wants to move to lane 'A'. There is a steady stream of traffic approaching (illustrated by the red dotted lines). Should the learner: (Tick the correct box.)

   Stop and wait at point 'C' for a suitable gap in the traffic?

   Continue in lane 'B' and match speed with traffic in lane 'A' before changing lanes?

3. Number the observation checks that the learner must make before changing lane.

   Interior mirror

   Right door mirror

   Left door mirror

   Right shoulder glance

   Left shoulder glance

   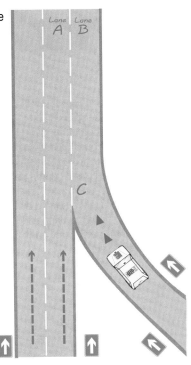

4. Are car drivers permitted to use the bus lane, controlled by the sign shown opposite, during the evening rush hour?

    ☐ Yes   ☐ No

5. The sign to the right means?

    ☐ Contra-flow bus lane.   ☐ With-flow bus lane.

6. You are approaching a queue of traffic. Draw a box to show where you would stop.

7. You are parked at the side of the road during rush hour and you want to move off. What would be the correct procedure to follow?

    ☐ Use your mirror, look over your right shoulder, wait for a gap and then signal to move away.

    ☐ Use your mirror, look over your right shoulder, signal (whether there's a gap or not) edge slightly forward and then wait for someone to let you in the stream of traffic.

8. To avoid the football traffic on a Saturday you need to take the next turning left. Draw two lines to show the path you would take.

9. You are on a one way street and you want to take the next turning on the left but you are concerned that the bus ahead may be on a collision course. What should you do?

☐ Speed up and get in front of the bus before the turning so that the driver of the bus knows to give way at the give way lines on the bus lane.

☐ Slow down and wait, if necessary, to allow the bus to proceed across the face of the junction first.

10. What do the yellow (Y) and white (W) hatch markings mean? Please place the letter Y and/or W next to the appropriate meaning:

☐ Only enter the marked area if you have a green light.

☐ Only enter the marked area if your exit is clear.

☐ Do not stop or wait on this area.

☐ Keep this area clear for crossing traffic.

Lesson 13 - Town and city centre driving

Lesson targets

At the end of the lesson tick those targets below that have been achieved. If any of the targets are ticked as completed with help, review them again after your next lesson.

Clutch Control

MSM Routine

...ination

	With help from my instructor	Without help from my instructor
I maintain all round awareness when in traffic queues or on multiple lane roads.	1	1
I show courtesy to other drivers and avoid blocking side roads.	2	2
I keep to my lane when turning and merging with traffic.	3	3
I can merge from the left and right safely.	4	4
I recognize at the earliest opportunity when I need to change lanes and change safely.	5	5
I recognize cycle, bus and tram lanes and act accordingly.	6	6
I recognize parking and traffic flow restrictions.	7	7
I feel comfortable driving in multiple lane one way systems.	8	8

Lesson 14 - Progressive driving

Introduction

Progressive driving is about making maximum progress for the road, traffic and weather conditions without risking safety. This requires more driving skill and better planning and awareness, particularly when you are overtaking or negotiating bends in the road.

Two of the most dangerous and difficult manoeuvres that you can undertake in driving are overtaking fast moving traffic on a two-way single carriageway and negotiating bends at speed. Therefore the aim of this lesson is to help you learn how to control the car at speed, negotiate bends and to overtake safely when the opportunity arises.

Lesson objectives

By the end of this lesson you should be able to:

- ► Explain the difference between progressive driving and speeding;
- ► explain the conditions that are likely to result in a skid and loss of control of the vehicle;
- ► consistently drive at such a speed that you can stop within the distance you can see to be clear;
- ► explain what factors need to be considered when assessing how fast a bend can safely be negotiated and the risks involved;
- ► identify the sharpness of a bend on approach and therefore the most suitable speed and gear to negotiate the bend;
- ► demonstrate a reasonable level of skill in negotiating bends of differing shapes and complexity;

- ► explain the likely places it would be unsafe to overtake and why;
- ► demonstrate a reasonable level of skill in overtaking moving vehicles at speed on a single two way carriageway.

Subject brief

Progressive driving is about making maximum progress for the road and weather conditions. It is about minimizing your journey time without risking safety. During this lesson you will learn, how to overtake fast moving vehicles on a single carriageway, how to negotiate bends at speed and also how to recognize when speed, can result in a waste of time, energy and fuel.

There is one golden rule about speed - never drive beyond the limits of your vision - always drive at such a speed that you can stop safely within the distance you can see to be clear.

Speed versus progress

Speed does not necessarily equal progress. For example when you are proceeding in a constant flow of traffic that has few significant gaps there is little point in racing to overtake at every opportunity you get as your progress will continually be hindered by the overall flow of the traffic.

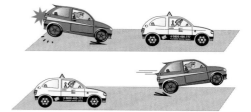

You would be constantly slowing down and accelerating throughout the journey to save a few minutes out of a 60 minute journey time. The fuel you would use on such a journey would potentially be doubled and your energy would be sapped from all the extra concentration you would need to cope with the overtaking and the constant changes of

speed. Therefore the progressive driver uses his or her brain and does not waste fuel or energy for little or no gain in overall journey times. One extra stop for fuel would loose any gain you might make.

Keeping a grip

When driving at speed road and tyre adhesion become critical. Therefore anything that will influence this adhesion must be considered when you are driving. Tyre tread, tyre pressure and the cars suspension all affect the cars ability to stop or take corners at speed.

Changes in the road surface also play a major role. Wet leaves, mud, oil, ice and water on the surface of the road all affect adhesion as does the actual material make up of the road surface itself. Certain road surface materials give a better grip. Changes in the way the road inclines can also affect adhesion particularly on corners. All the above need to be carefully considered if you want to make maximum progress without compromising safety.

Driving round the bend

There is a lot of skill and balance needed to make maximum progress round bends. However, the first thing to remember is the golden rule. Just because you can take a bend at 50 mph doesn't mean that you should, especially, if you cannot see what's around the corner. You may discover a steam roller, a combine harvester or an articulated lorry waiting for you!

When approaching a bend you need to consider; the shape of the bend, what you can see ahead, what's on the roads surface (and does it incline in anyway) and finally what you will hit if you lose

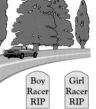

control. If there are trees along the road and you are pushing the car and/or your own ability to its limits then you are dicing with death. Bends take many "boy and girl racers" lives.

Balance

The first thing that you need to learn to successfully negotiate bends at speed is balance. The vehicle achieves maximum adhesion when the weight of the car is evenly spread over each wheel and across the whole of the tread of the tyres . As soon as you brake or turn the weight of the car shifts such that adhesion may primarily be occurring on only one or two of the wheels tyres and, if the wheels lock, only across part of the tyres tread. This dramatically increases the risk of a skid (i.e. the loss of adhesion) and makes the car very unstable. Therefore you should not be braking or accelerating at the point you enter the bend. Ideally you should maintain a constant speed into and around the bend. As you come out of the bend you can begin to accelerate.

Sensitivity

When you turn your steering wheel it should be done gradually and smoothly without jerking. You are trying to minimize the sharpness of the curve you are turning without cutting across to the other side of the road or allowing your road position to become a hazard to oncoming vehicles. On approach to the hazard (i.e. the bend) you should properly apply your hazard drill making sure you are at the right speed and gear before you start to turn.

Overtaking at speed on single carriageways

Overtaking moving vehicles at speed on a single carriageway is potentially the most dangerous manoeuvre you can perform. You are driving on the wrong side of the road while traffic may be heading towards you.

60 MPH

120 MPH
Closing Gap
58.66 meters per second
or

14 car lengths per second

Choosing a safe place to overtake

Perhaps the most important thing to learn about overtaking is where not to overtake. You should never normally overtake immediately after a warning sign, in particular if it is one of those shown opposite:

You need to look well ahead for these hazards and road markings.

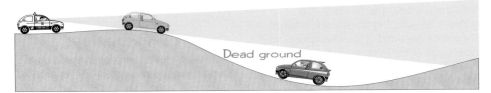

Dead ground

One physical hazard that is not easy to spot is something termed "Dead Ground". This is where the road dips into a hollow such that it can give you the illusion that there are no oncoming vehicles when in fact there are.

There are two important points to learn from this. Firstly, if your view ahead is not absolutely clear wait and secondly; always be prepared to brake and abort the overtake, if necessary.

Never `follow through`

You may occasionally find yourself in a stream of vehicles, all of which intend to overtake a slow moving vehicle. Make sure that you can see clearly ahead before overtaking in this situation. Never 'blindly' follow the vehicle ahead assuming that it is safe.

The overtaking procedure

The overtaking procedure is similar to that covered on the dual carriageway lesson, however, we now have to consider oncoming traffic. Again you would probably use the hazard drill at least 3 times as shown opposite:

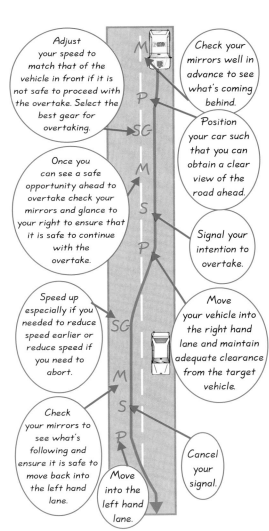

Adjust your speed to match that of the vehicle in front if it is not safe to proceed with the overtake. Select the best gear for overtaking.

Check your mirrors well in advance to see what's coming behind.

M

P

SG

Position your car such that you can obtain a clear view of the road ahead.

Once you can see a safe opportunity ahead to overtake check your mirrors and glance to your right to ensure that it is safe to continue with the overtake.

M

S

P

Signal your intention to overtake.

Speed up especially if you needed to reduce speed earlier or reduce speed if you need to abort.

SG

M

Move your vehicle into the right hand lane and maintain adequate clearance from the target vehicle.

S

Check your mirrors to see what's following and ensure it is safe to move back into the left hand lane.

P

Move into the left hand lane.

Cancel your signal.

132

Lesson quiz

1. You are overtaking traffic at 60 MPH and you are not sure that you can make it. What should you do?

☐ Flash your headlights to warn the oncoming vehicle to slow down.

☐ Indicate left to warn the car on your left that you propose to cut in.

☐ Brake harshly and abandon the overtake manoeuvre.

☐ Speed up and break the speed limit in an attempt to beat the oncoming car.

2. Tick what you think would have possibly contributed to the problem above.

☐ You misjudged either the distance or the speed of the approaching vehicle.

☐ The driver approaching was definitely breaking the speed limit.

☐ You did not see the car in front of the lorry until it was too late.

☐ The driver of the car to your left speeded up.

☐ The lorry was too close to the car in front.

☐ The road surface was slippery and prevented you from accelerating.

3. What is the national speed limit for cars on single carriageways ?

☐ 50 MPH ☐ 60 MPH ☐ 70 MPH

4. Assuming that your skill, the road surface and the car could enable you to take this bend at 60 MPH at what speed should you be travelling at point A and then at point B (assuming that at point B the road ahead is straight and clear). Place A or B next to the appropriate speed.

☐ 60 MPH

☐ 50 MPH

☐ 30 MPH

5. On the diagram above draw two lines to show the approximate path of the front wheels of the car as you negotiate this bend.

6. In the above situation what road surface hazard might you encounter in autumn that does not occur at other times of the year.

☐

7. Assuming that you could see that there were no oncoming vehicles can you overtake the vehicle ahead in any of the following situations?

A)

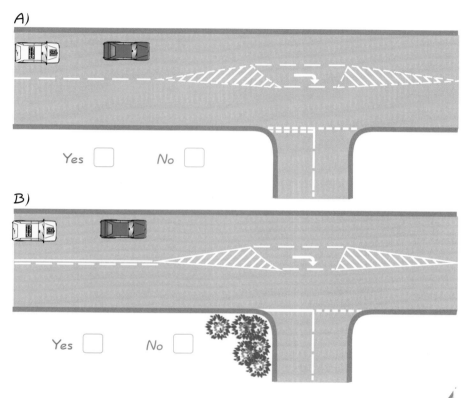

Yes ☐   No ☐

B)

Yes ☐   No ☐

8. You come across a slow moving vehicle travelling at about 5 MPH. You cannot overtake the vehicle without crossing the unbroken white line ahead. However, you believe you can see sufficiently ahead not to endanger oncoming vehicles. What should you do?

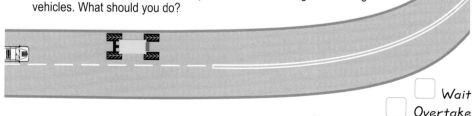

☐ Wait
☐ Overtake

9. You see a car illegally parked at the side of the road. What should you do?

☐ Overtake with extreme care.

☐ Stop behind the car and find out why it has stopped.

10. In the above example draw two lines to show the path of the front wheels of the car if you decided to overtake the parked car or a box to show where you would park depending upon which of the options you choose.

11. In the road situations below who has priority over the central overtaking lane. Does the vehicle from the left have:

A)   Equal priority?
B)   Secondary priority?
C)   Cannot use the overtaking lane at all?

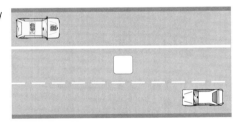

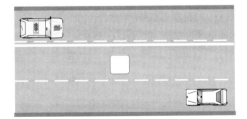

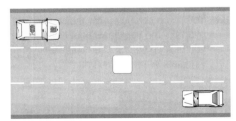

12. If you were to guess, how far do you think the road ahead would need to be clear and remain clear for you to safely overtake the green car if you were travelling at 60 mph and the green car was travelling at 40 mph?

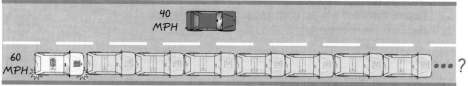

20.97 car lengths (83.88 metres)

13.93 car lengths (55.72 metres)

5.00 car lengths (20 metres)

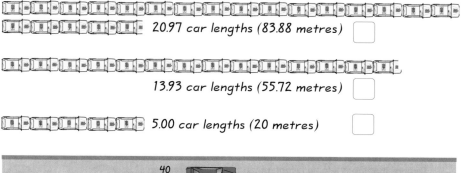

For those who do not want to guess:

At 20mph (i.e the difference in speed between you and the green car) it will take approximately 3.13 seconds (at 2.23 car lengths per second) to complete the overtake manoeuvre therefore at 60mph (i.e. 6.7 car lengths per second) how far will the overtaking car have traveled in 3.13 seconds?

Lesson targets

At the end of the lesson tick those targets below that have been achieved. If any of the targets are ticked as completed with help, review them again after your next lesson.

Clutch Control ✓
MSM Routine ✓
...ination ✓

Overtaking

	With help from my instructor	Without help from my instructor

Before I overtake I:

Apply the hazard drill on approach; take up a good position to maximize my view ahead and select the best gear for acceleration. ① ①

Carefully consider the safety of the location. (Is this stretch of road suitable?) ② ②

Ensure that there is a sufficient gap in the traffic ahead so that I can return to the left. ③ ③

Assess whether I can reach the gap on the left well before any oncoming vehicles (seen or unseen). ④ ④

When overtaking I:

Use my mirrors and glance to my right before pulling out. ⑤ ⑤

Move over to the right and make a final check ahead before I proceed. ⑥ ⑥

Accelerate briskly to pass the 'target' vehicle(s) as quickly as possible. ⑦ ⑦

Move back to the left safely without 'cutting in'. ⑧ ⑧

Making progress

I make maximum progress for the weather, road and traffic conditions. ⑨ ⑨

Lesson targets (continued)

Negotiating bends

	With help from my instructor	Without help from my instructor

Before I reach the bend I determine the speed and therefore the gear needed to safely negotiate the bend by considering:

	With help from my instructor	Without help from my instructor
What I see of the road ahead to be clear.	10	10
The shape of the bend.	11	11
The road surface of the bend.	12	12
What would happen if I lost control.	13	13
Whether my intended road position would present a hazard to oncoming traffic.	14	14

As I negotiate the bend I:

Select the appropriate gear early.	15	15
Maintain a constant speed.	16	16
Steer with both hands using a smooth action.	17	17
Maintain a safe road position throughout.	18	18

Lesson 15 - The driving test

Introduction

You have now completed the programme and should have the necessary driving skills to pass the UK driving test. However, before you take the test it's important that you understand how the test works so that you do not get any surprises on the day. To do this your instructor will simulate a full driving test and act like an examiner. Therefore the purpose of this lesson is to make you comfortable with the driving test itself and identify any final driving weaknesses you may have.

Lesson objectives

By the end of this lesson you should be able to:

- Identify the three categories of driving fault that may occur on the driving test;
- assess the outcome of your driving test from the marking sheet provided;
- explain the procedure that is likely to be followed on the day of the test;
- identify any remaining driving weaknesses.

Subject brief

The Driving Standards Agency driving test for car drivers is about 40 minutes long. During this time the examiner will expect you to satisfy the eyesight test, show and tell him how to undertake certain vehicle safety checks and demonstrate an ability to drive the car safely around a given test route. The route will encompass a wide variety of different road conditions and at various points along the way the examiner will also require you to complete certain test manoeuvres. In particular you will be required to undertake two of the following set manoeuvres and optionally the emergency stop:

Reverse parking behind a parked car or into a parking bay; reversing round a corner to either the left or right; turn in the road.

Driving on the test is a little different from driving with your driving instructor on a driving lesson. The most obvious difference is that the examiner is not going to help you with your driving or your answers to the "show me tell me" part of the test. However, the examiner will be happy to clarify any instruction he or she may have given to you. The examiner will also try to put you at ease, as the last thing that they what is to make you feel unnecessarily anxious or uncomfortable. The examiner wants to test your driving ability not your nerve.

Therefore don't be surprised at how friendly they are. You may find that your examiner offers encouragement or advice with regard to your test nerves. Once the examiner has introduced him or her self he or she will ask you to read a number plate at the required distance. Assuming that you are able to do this, the examiner will ask you to take him or her to your vehicle where he or she will check its condition before entering the vehicle. At this point the examiner will ask you two questions, one 'show me' and one 'tell me'. One or both questions answered incorrectly will result in one minor driving fault being recorded. If the "show me" question requires you to open the bonnet this question will be asked before you get into the vehicle otherwise the "show me tell me" part of the test will commence after you have entered the vehicle.

Next you start the driving part of the driving test. While still in the car park the examiner may ask you to pull forward and complete the bay park exercise otherwise you will be asked to move away when it is safe to do so. The examiner will give you route directions in good time. If you go the wrong way do not panic the examiner is testing your ability to drive not your ability to follow directions. It is better to go the wrong way correctly than to go the right way incorrectly. If at any time you are unsure what the examiner requires do not hesitate to check what he or she wants; the examiner appreciates that you may be nervous and will be happy to repeat or clarify any instructions given. At certain points on the route the examiner may ask you to complete a set manoeuvre.

As soon you are asked to move off the examiner will start to assess your driving ability, noting any driving faults you may commit on the Driving Test Report – the DL25.

There are three types of driving fault that you can commit – minor, serious or dangerous. A serious or a dangerous fault will result in a test failure. An accumulation of more than 15 minor driving faults will also result in a test failure.

If a minor fault is committed the examiner denotes this by a '/' slash in the first box against the appropriate report heading. At the end of the test the examiner will use the second box to denote the total number of minor driving faults against that heading. If a serious fault is committed the examiner will denote this by placing a '/' in the third box against the appropriate heading. Finally, if a dangerous fault is committed the examiner will denote this by placing a '/' in the fourth box against the appropriate heading.

A dangerous fault results in test failure because the examiner or another road user had been forced to take evasive action to avoid an accident.

A serious fault also results in test failure because the fault affected another road user or had the potential to affect another road user.

A minor fault does not result in a test failure because it would not normally cause an accident but could be a contributing factor in certain circumstances. Fifteen or more such faults would suggest that the candidate was lucky not to have committed a serious or dangerous fault and should therefore fail the test. On the following pages you will see a list of common faults recorded by examiners under each of the headings shown. Use this as a guide to help you determine what, if any, driving weaknesses you may still have.

Common Driving Faults

Unable to enter side road.
Too far from kerb at completion.
Car not parallel to the kerb.

WITH PROPER OBSERVATION:
Does not look out of rear window.
Does not take all around observation throughout.
Uses nearside door mirror for observation.
Does not observe other road users.
Does not give way to other road users.
Does not pull forwards to allow vehicle to emerge from the side road.

1. COMPLY WITH
   REQUIREMENTS
   OF EYESIGHT TEST:
Unable to read a number plate at 67 feet or 20.5 meters which is about five car lengths.

2. CONTROLLED STOP.
   STOP THE VEHICLE IN AN EMERGENCY:
PROMPTLY:
Slow reaction to signal.
Not stopping quickly enough.

UNDER CONTROL:
Uses foot brake and clutch together.
Clutch pedal used too soon.
Harsh application of foot brake.
Uses handbrake to stop.
Locks front or rear wheels.
Induces a skid by braking and steering at the same time.
Loses control by skidding.

3&4. REVERSE INTO A LIMITED
     OPENING TO THE RIGHT OR LEFT:
UNDER CONTROL:
Poor Clutch control.
Stalls the engine.
Excessive acceleration.
Foot brake not used when required.
Erratic use of steering.
Touches kerb.
Mounts pavement.
Over centre of the side road.

5. REVERSE PARK:
UNDER CONTROL:
Poor clutch control.
Stalls the engine.
Excessive acceleration.
Insufficient or excessive steering.
Harsh use of foot brake.
Too close to parked car.
Strikes the kerb with front or rear nearside wheel.
Too far away from the left hand kerb at completion.
Car finishes up at an angle to the kerb.
Unable to complete within two car lengths.

WITH PROPER OBSERVATION:
Does not take all round observation before exercise.
Does not look out of the rear window while reversing.
Uses door mirror to observe while reversing.
Ignores passing traffic and does not give way.
Reverses back with pedestrians passing by on the pavement at rear.

6. TURN IN THE ROAD:
UNDER CONTROL:
Poor clutch control.
Stalls the engine.
Excessive acceleration.
Harsh use of foot brake.
Not applying the handbrake properly.
Strikes kerbs with front or rear wheels.

Mounts pavement with front or rear wheels.
Overhangs the kerb with front or rear of car.
Unable to complete exercise within five moves.
Turns the steering wheel in the wrong direction.
No attempt to correct steering on forward or reverse moves.

WITH PROPER OBSERVATION:

Lack of all round observation before moving.
Moves forwards or backwards when unsafe to do so.
Does not look to the rear while reversing.
Only looks back over one shoulder while reversing.
Lack of all round observation during each movement.
Continues with movement, does not give way to passing traffic.
Does not allow pedestrians to proceed safely on the pavements.

7.   VEHICLE CHECKS
Show me tell me part

11.   TAKE PRECAUTIONS BEFORE STARTING THE ENGINE:

Jumping forward while attempting to start the engine with the car in gear.

Rolling backwards or forwards while attempting to restart the engine.

12.   CONTROLS, MAKE PROPER USE OF:
ACCELERATOR:
Excessive pressure causing wheel spin.
Erratic pressure causing surging.
Not removing pressure while changing gear.
Applying pressure too soon after changing gear.

CLUTCH:
Jerky control.
Lack of control.
Releases too quickly.
Riding the pedal.
Not pressing fully to the floor.
Not used when stopping.

GEARS:
Incorrect gear selection.
Reluctant to select higher gears.
Labours the engine.
Does not match gear with road speed.
Excessive speed in gear.
Unnecessary gear changes.
Used to reduce speed instead of brakes.
Selected too soon for hazards.
Selected too late for hazards.
Coasting with clutch down.
Coasting in neutral.

FOOT BRAKE:
Not used when required.
Late use on approach to hazards.
Harsh use by pressing too fiercely.

HANDBRAKE:
Not applying when necessary.
Not releasing properly.
Moving away with it partially on.
Not applying properly.
Applying on the move.
Rolling backwards or forwards after stopping.

STEERING:
Incorrect hand position on the wheel.
Losing control by crossing hands.
Allowing wheel to spin back after turning.
Retaining hand on the gear lever for too long.
Removes both hands from steering wheel.
Overshooting right turns.
Over steers on corners.
Under steers on corners.
Steering with the right arm on the window ledge.
Striking the kerb when stopping.

13.   MOVE AWAY:
SAFELY:
No attempt to look around.
Lack of observation ahead and to the rear.
Moves away when unsafe.

UNDER CONTROL:
Stalls the engine.
Moving away at too high a speed.
Rolls back.

14. MAKE EFFECTIVE USE OF MIRROR(S) WELL BEFORE:

SIGNALLING:
Does not use Mirror Signal Manoeuvre routine.
Signals before using mirrors.
Looks and signals at the same time.
Does not take appropriate action after observing traffic in mirrors.
Signals regardless of following traffic situation.

CHANGING DIRECTION:
Does not consult mirrors before turning left.
Does not consult mirrors before turning right.
Does not consult mirrors before changing lanes.
Does not consult mirrors before overtaking.
Does not consult mirrors after overtaking.

CHANGING SPEED:
Does not consult mirrors before increasing speed.
Does not consult mirrors before reducing speed.
Does not consult mirrors before stopping.

15. GIVE SIGNALS:

WHERE NECESSARY:
Omits signals when they could benefit other road users.

CORRECTLY:
Gives signals in the wrong direction.
Gives misleading signals.
Does not cancel signals after completion of manoeuvre.
Using any signal not in the highway code.

PROPERLY TIMED:
Give signals too early.
Gives signals too late.
Signals for too short a period of time.
Signals for too long a period of time.

16. ALLOW ADEQUATE CLEARANCE TO STATIONARY VEHICLES:

Drives too close to the rear of stationary vehicles before pulling out.

Drives too close to the side of stationary vehicles while driving past.
Cuts back to the left too soon after passing stationary vehicles.

17 RESPOND TO SIGNS/SIGNALS:

TRAFFIC SIGNS:
Disregards speed limit signs.
Does not obey mandatory signs.
Ignores prohibiting signs.
Ignores warning signs.

ROAD MARKINGS:
Does not act in accordance with lane direction arrows.
Crosses or straddles double white lines.
Drives in bus lanes at prohibited times.
Parks on double yellow lines.
Disregards box junction markings.
Stops on worded markings such as "Keep Clear".
Parks on zig-zag lines.

TRAFFIC LIGHTS:
Attempts to drive through a Red light.
Does not stop on Amber when it was safe to do so.
Drives away on Red and Amber.
Proceeds on green light when unsafe to do so.

TRAFFIC CONTROLLERS:
Disregards signals given by police or a traffic warden.
Disregards signals given by a person in charge of road works with Stop/Go sign.
Disregards signal given by School Crossing Patrol.

OTHER ROAD USERS:
Disregards clearly given signals by other drivers.

18. EXERCISE PROPER CARE IN THE USE OF SPEED:

Drives in excess of the speed limit.
Drives at a speed which is too fast for the road and traffic conditions.

19. FOLLOW BEHIND ANOTHER
    VEHICLE AT A SAFE DISTANCE:
Drives too close to large vehicles ahead.
Does not adopt the two second rule.
Drives closer than thinking distance in heavy
traffic.
Stops too close to vehicles ahead in traffic
queues.

20. MAKES PROGRESS BY:
DRIVING AT A SPEED APPROPRIATE TO THE
ROAD AND TRAFFIC CONDITIONS:
Crawls along at slow speeds on clear roads.
Makes no attempt to achieve maximum speeds
for the road when safe to do so.
Reduces speed excessively when the conditions
do not merit doing so.
Makes slow progress through the gears in normal
driving.

AVOIDING UNDUE HESITANCY:
Makes predetermined stops at junctions and
other hazards.
Waits unnecessarily when it is safe to proceed at
junctions.
Waits for Green light at Pedestrian Crossings
when clear on flashing amber.
Waits for other drivers, who are clearly giving
way.

21. ACT PROPERLY AT ROAD JUNCTION
    WITH REGARD TO:
SPEED ON APPROACH:
Approaches at too high a speed.
Approaches at too slow a speed.

OBSERVATION:
Only looks in one direction at junctions before
emerging.
Looks in both directions after emerging.
Does not look in the direction of travel while
emerging.
Takes no observation whatsoever at unmarked
crossroads.
Emerges at too slow a speed.
Emerges when traffic is too close or too fast.
Emerges into the path of approaching traffic.

POSITION BEFORE TURNING RIGHT:
Positions over centre lines.
Positions left of centre in narrow roads.
Does not position near enough to centre lines.
Does not move into protected centre lane.
Does not use right hand lane, when one is
available.
Does not proceed far enough forward when
giving way to oncoming traffic.
Does not move out to centre of the side road
when turning right at traffic lights.
Sits behind stop line at green light, with room to
move forwards.

POSITION BEFORE TURNING LEFT:
Too far from left hand kerb on the approach.
Swings out to the right on the approach.
Too close to the kerb on approach.
Drives over the kerb with rear nearside wheel.

CUTTING RIGHT HAND CORNERS:
Cuts across onto the wrong side of side road
while turning the corner.

22. JUDGEMENT, DEAL WITH OTHER
    VEHICLES SAFELY WHEN:
OVERTAKING:
Attempts to overtake in an unsafe location.
Attempts to overtake when traffic conditions make
it unsafe to do so.
Takes too long a time and distance to carry out
manoeuvre.
Does not give enough clearance to other
vehicles.
Cuts back in too soon after overtaking.

MEETING:
Causes oncoming traffic to slow down or stop.
Drives on towards other vehicles when other
vehicles have priority.

CROSSING THEIR PATH:
Inconveniences oncoming road users by cutting
across in front of them.

23. POSITION THE VEHICLE CORRECTLY: DURING NORMAL DRIVING:

Drives too close to the left hand kerb.
Drives too far out towards the middle of the road.

EXERCISE LANE DISCIPLINE:

Chooses incorrect lane when proceeding ahead at roundabouts or traffic lights.
Straddles lane markings.
Wanders back and forwards from one lane to the other.

24. TAKES APPROPRIATE ACTION AT PEDESTRIAN CROSSINGS:

Does not reduce speed on the approach when vision is restricted.
Approaches at too high a speed with pedestrians on crossing.
Overtaking on Zig-Zag lines on approach.
Not giving precedence to pedestrians on a crossing.
Not stopping at give way or stop lines when necessary.
Not acting in accordance with the traffic lights controlling the crossing.
Harassing pedestrians.
Waving pedestrians over a crossing.
Moving away before pedestrians have crossed over in front of the car.
Attempting to proceed when unsafe to do so.
Stopping on the actual crossing.

25. SELECT A SAFE POSITION FOR NORMAL STOPS:

Stopping in an unsafe or inconvenient location.
Blocking an entrance or driveway when stopping.
Causing an obstruction to other road users..
Stopping too far away from the pavement.
Stopping with one or more wheels on the pavement.

26. SHOW AWARENESS AND ANTICIPATION OF THE ACTIONS OF:

OTHER ROAD USERS:

Not anticipating that pedestrians are about to cross the road at any time.
Not giving way to pedestrians at junctions or pedestrian crossings.
Not anticipating that cyclists may be passing on the left or right.
Not anticipating that cyclists are about to make a change of direction.
Not anticipating or showing awareness of direction signals given by other drivers.
Not anticipating or showing awareness of vehicles displaying hazard flashers.
Not anticipating or showing awareness of vehicles reversing lights.
Not anticipating or showing awareness of brake lights on other vehicles.
Not anticipating the actions of other drivers changing speed or direction.

27. USE OF ANCILLARY CONTROLS

Only applicable if driver requires to use them in addition to the normal controls.
Not operating the front or rear windscreen wipers or washers when required.
Not operating the side or headlamp controls when required.
Not operating the horn when required.
Not operating the heated rear screen control when required.
Not operating the demister controls when required.
Not operating the hazard warning lights when required.

Marking Sheet

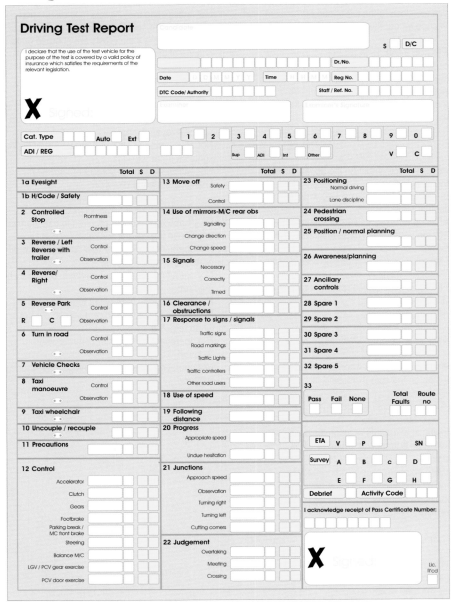

Driving Test Report

Candidate

S | D/C

I declare that the use of the test vehicle for the purpose of the test is covered by a valid policy of insurance which satisfies the requirements of the relevant legislation.

Dr./No.

Date | Time | Reg No.

DTC Code/ Authority | Staff / Ref. No.

X Signed:

| Cat. Type | | Auto | Ext | | 1 | 2 | 3 | 4 | 5 | 6 | 7 | 8 | 9 | 0 |

| ADI / REG | | | | | | Sup | ADI | Int | Other | | V | C |

	Total S D		Total S D		Total S D
1a Eyesight		**13 Move off** Safety		**23 Positioning** Normal driving	
1b H/Code / Safety		Control		Lane discipline	
2 Controlled Stop Promtness		**14 Use of mirrrors-M/C rear obs**		**24 Pedestrian crossing**	
Control		Signalling			
		Change direction		**25 Position / normal planning**	
3 Reverse / Left Reverse with trailer Control		Change speed			
Observation		**15 Signals** Necessary		**26 Awareness/planning**	
4 Reverse/ Right Control		Correctly		**27 Ancillary controls**	
Observation		Timed			
5 Reverse Park Control		**16 Clearance / obstructions**		**28 Spare 1**	
R C Observation		**17 Response to signs / signals**		**29 Spare 2**	
6 Turn in road Control		Traffic signs		**30 Spare 3**	
Observation		Road markings		**31 Spare 4**	
7 Vehicle Checks		Traffic Lights		**32 Spare 5**	
8 Taxi manoeuvre Control		Traffic controllers			
Observation		Other road users		**33**	
9 Taxi wheelchair		**18 Use of speed**		Pass Fail None	Total Faults / Route no
10 Uncouple / recouple		**19 Following distance**			
11 Precautions		**20 Progress** Appropriate speed		ETA V P SN	
12 Control		Undue hesitation		Survey A B C D	
Accelerator		**21 Junctions** Approach speed		E F G H	
Clutch		Observation		**Debrief** **Activity Code**	
Gears		Turning right		I acknowledge receipt of Pass Certificate Number:	
Footbrake		Turning left			
Parking break / MC front brake		Cutting corners			
Steering		**22 Judgement** Overtaking		**X** Signed:	Lic. R'cd
Balance M/C		Meeting			
LGV / PCV gear exercise		Crossing			
PCV door exercise					

Introduction

Once you have developed the main foundation skills going forwards you can begin to develop them going backwards starting with the straight-line reverse. The reversing lessons can be introduced into the programme at any point after the co-ordination lesson and can be combined with one or more of the forward driving lessons. However, it is important that each of the reversing manoeuvres is learnt in the order shown as the skills learnt in the first manoeuvres lesson become the sub skills for the next and so on. All the reversing manoeuvres should be undertaken in quiet housing estates or car parks.

Lesson Objectives

By the end of this lesson you should be able to:

- ► explain about the use of seat belts during reversing;
- ► explain the importance of selecting a safe, legal and convenient place when undertaking any reversing manoeuvre;
- ► select reverse gear; sit correctly to enable effective rear observations;
- ► hold the steering wheel correctly with your right hand at the 12 o'clock position;
- ► explain why there is a delayed action when steering while reversing;
- ► maintain a straight course;
- ► use clutch control to maintain a slow speed;
- ► pause periodically in order to maintain all round observations throughout the manoeuvre;

- ► deal correctly with other road users while reversing;
- ► complete the exercise on roads with varying gradients.

Subject brief

Straight line reversing is the first set manoeuvre you need to learn. It forms the basis for all the other manoeuvres you may encounter on the test. The key points are:

1. Location
   Make sure that where you intend to reverse is safe, legal and convenient.

2. Seating position and seatbelt
   When reversing you can unfasten your seatbelt to enable you to shuffle around in your seat so that you can look through the rear window by looking over your left shoulder.

3. Hand(s) position on the steering wheel
   When reversing you would usually hold the steering wheel with the right hand at the 12 o'clock position and, optionally, the left hand at the 6 o'clock position.

4. Select reverse gear
   If this wasn't covered in earlier lessons you will be shown how to select reverse.

5. Low speed - clutch control
    All the set manoeuvres
    should be undertaken at
    a very slow speed
    by using what
    is termed "clutch
    control".

    Slow is beautiful

    Pause occasionally and look all around

6. All round awareness
    While reversing
    you should be
    taking
    observations
    through the rear
    window of the vehicle occasionally
    pausing using clutch control to take all
    round observations.

7. Look well back for positioning
    In exactly the same way that you
    position the car when moving forward
    by looking well ahead (i.e. where you
    want to go) the same is true for driving
    in reverse. The near side door mirror
    may also be useful for checking the
    position of the vehicle in relation to the
    kerb.

8. Dealing with other road users
    When reversing pause and wait if a
    vehicle appears to your rear.
    Particularly watch for pedestrians or
    children on bikes crossing to your rear.
    Again you need to give way and wait.
    When crossing a driveway to your rear
    watch for road users emerging from or
    wanting to turn into the driveway.

Lesson quiz

1. When reversing, you need to maintain all around observation to ensure safety. Apart from this, your observation will help you to position the car. Where should you look, in order to steer the car in a straight line, when reversing? (Tick two correct answers.)

- [ ] At the kerb.
- [ ] At the nearside mirror.
- [ ] Well back along the road.
- [ ] At the steering wheel.
- [ ] Out of the rear window.

2. When reversing you may remove your seatbelt.

   True: [ ]   *False:* [ ]

3. When reversing in a straight line you may sometimes steer with one hand only. Mark the steering wheel to show where you would position your hand for 'one-hand' steering.

   Which hand would you use? [ ]

4. The Highway Code explains the importance of making sure that there are no pedestrians or obstructions in the 'blind spots' around your vehicle Imagine that you are sitting in the car below; shade in the areas around the car that you (sitting in the driving seat and looking around through the rear window) will not be able to see clearly.

5. Write 'a', 'b' or 'c', in the box below, as the advice given by The Highway Code to drivers who cannot see clearly behind their vehicle when reversing.

    a. Drive very slowly to minimise the damage if you hit something.

    b. Get someone to guide you.

    c. Don't reverse too far.

    Which? ▢

6. You are about to reverse, what order would you complete the following actions?

    B. Take up seating position and place right hand on steering wheel.

    C. Check all round and release hand brake.

    A. Clutch down and select reverse gear

    Order? ▢▢▢

7. In the examples below you want the car to reduce speed to slow walking pace. Place the letter A, B or C to denote which method you would use in the following situations:

    A. Depress the clutch slightly while applying extra acceleration.

    B. Depress the clutch slightly while braking.

    C. Depress the clutch slightly while applying normal acceleration.

Lesson targets

At the end of the lesson tick those targets below that have been achieved. If any of the targets are ticked as completed with help, review them again after your next lesson.

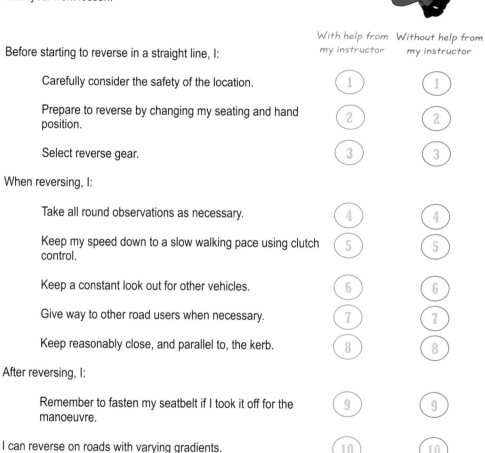

	With help from my instructor	Without help from my instructor
Before starting to reverse in a straight line, I:		
Carefully consider the safety of the location.	1	1
Prepare to reverse by changing my seating and hand position.	2	2
Select reverse gear.	3	3
When reversing, I:		
Take all round observations as necessary.	4	4
Keep my speed down to a slow walking pace using clutch control.	5	5
Keep a constant look out for other vehicles.	6	6
Give way to other road users when necessary.	7	7
Keep reasonably close, and parallel to, the kerb.	8	8
After reversing, I:		
Remember to fasten my seatbelt if I took it off for the manoeuvre.	9	9
I can reverse on roads with varying gradients.	10	10

Introduction

Once you have mastered the skill of reversing in a straight line you will be ready to undertake the more difficult skill of reversing round a corner or into a parking bay. The reverse round a corner is basically made up of two straight-line reverses with a turn in between. Therefore the extra skills needed relate to the steering and the additional observational checks needed before, during and after the turn. These skills will also enable you to reverse into a parking bay or driveway.

Lesson Objectives

By the end of this lesson you should be able to:

► Explain when it would not be safe, legal or convenient to carry out this manoeuvre;

► pull up in a suitable position on the left hand side of the road just after the side road into which you intend to reverse;

► explain the dangers caused by the car as you start to turn;

► judge when you should begin to turn depending on the sharpness of the corner;

► make suitable observational checks throughout the manoeuvre and especially before you turn, ensuring it is safe to proceed;

► steer a suitable course as you turn and keep within a metre of the kerb or less if the road is narrow or within the parking bay lines when parking;

► judge when you should begin to straighten up your steering as you enter the side road or the parking bay;

► correct positioning errors;

► deal correctly with other road users;

► recognise when you have reversed far enough into the side road for the driving test;

► complete the exercise on sharp and curved corners on roads with and without gradients;

► remember to fasten your seat belt before driving away safely.

Subject brief

Reversing to the left forms part of everyday driving for many motorists.

Turning around

The safest and easiest way to turn around and go back in the opposite direction is to drive all the way around a roundabout or around the block.

If this is not possible, the next best, and most common, solution, is to reverse into an opening on the left.

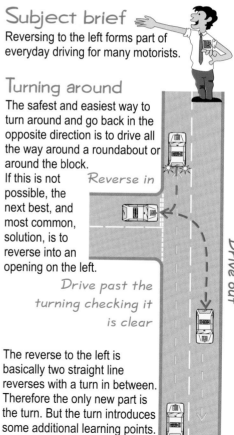

Reverse in

Drive past the turning checking it is clear

Drive out

The reverse to the left is basically two straight line reverses with a turn in between. Therefore the only new part is the turn. But the turn introduces some additional learning points.

1. Location

You must never reverse from a side road into the main road. You would only consider reversing into a side road on the left that was a give way junction and had little or no traffic emerging out of it. Again you would need to consider whether it was legal, safe or convenient.

2. Hand(s) position on the steering wheel

At the point you start to turn you will need to use both hands and the pull push method of steering although it may be offset to the left so that you can maintain observations over you left shoulder.

When looking to the rear the effect of turning the steering wheel on the vehicles position is much less pronounced (because there is no bonnet to act like a guns sights). The effects of steering also appear to be delayed. This is why it is easy to oversteer when reversing.

3. All round awareness

Because you intend to turn into a side road against the flow of traffic extra observations are needed into the side road. Extra observations are also needed to the front as the front of the

car will swing out as you turn and may present a hazard to passing traffic on the major road.

4. Dealing with other road users

When reversing to the left be prepared to abandon the manoeuvre and drive forward to the start position. Until you are well back into the side road, it is potentially very dangerous for other vehicles to overtake you so close to the junction.

5. Distance you need to reverse into the side road

When reversing to the left on test you are required to reverse back for a reasonable distance (i.e. about 3 to 4 car lengths) into the side road.

Lesson quiz

1. If another vehicle approaches while you are reversing into a side road you should:

☐ Always give way.

☐ Be prepared to give way.

☐ Reverse quickly to get out of the way.

2. Which of the following pictures show the correct way to reverse to the left?

Which is correct? (1,2,3 or 4) ☐

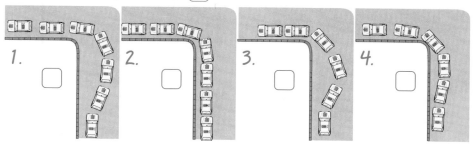

1. ☐ 2. ☐ 3. ☐ 4. ☐

Now write 'a', 'b' or 'c', in the relevant green box, to show why the other manoeuvres are wrong.

a: Began to turn too late.
b: Began to steer too soon.
c: Started to turn at the right time but failed to turn the wheel enough.

Now on the above diagram that shows the correct reverse to the left write the letter "O" at the point or points where you would definitely take all round observations before proceeding.

3. Complete the following sentences:

The Highway Code states that you should never reverse from a s.........................
r......................... into a m......................... r......................... . In addition, it also says that you
should avoid r......................... into a road from a driveway.

4. What would you do in the following situations? Would you continue with the manoeuvre,
wait or pull forward? Assume that there are no other vehicles around and that all the
junctions are open.

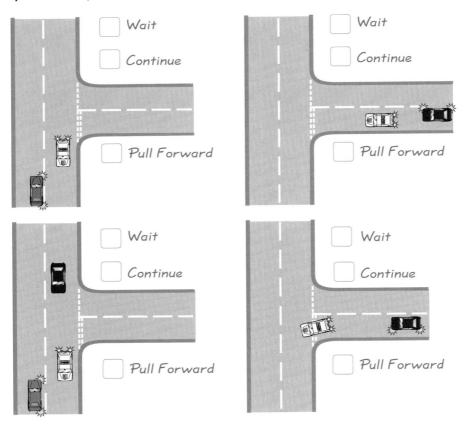

Lesson targets

At the end of the lesson tick those targets below that have been achieved. If any of the targets are ticked as completed with help, review them again after your next lesson.

Clutch Control ✓
MSM Routine ✓
...dination ✓

	With help from my instructor	Without help from my instructor
Before starting to manoeuvre, I:		
Carefully consider whether the location is safe, legal or convenient.	1	1
Make sure that the side road is clear and that it is safe to reverse into it.	2	2
When reversing, I:		
Keep my speed down to a slow walking pace.	3	3
Keep a constant look out for other vehicles.	4	4
Give way to other road users and pull forward when necessary.	5	5
Finish up reasonably close, and parallel to, the kerb.	6	6
After reversing, I:		
Remember to fasten my seatbelt if I took it off for the manoeuvre.	7	7

M3 - Reversing to the right

Introduction

Once you have mastered the skill of reversing round a corner or into a parking bay on your left it's time for you to learn how to do this from the right. These lessons can often be combined because of the similarity between the two skills. The main difference being that the kerb is on your right hand side, which requires you to alternate between looking over your left and your right hand shoulder.

Lesson Objectives

By the end of this lesson you should be able to:

- ► Explain when it would not be safe, legal or convenient to carry out this manoeuvre;
- ► explain the dangers caused by the car as you start to turn;
- ► pull up in a suitable position on the right hand side of the road just after the side road into which you intend to reverse, timing your signal correctly;
- ► judge when you should begin to turn depending on the sharpness of the corner;
- ► correctly switch your seating position and the position of your hands to take observations to the rear over your right shoulder as you negotiate the corner;
- ► make suitable all round observational checks throughout the manoeuvre and especially before you turn, ensuring it is safe to proceed;
- ► steer a suitable course as you turn and keep within a metre of the kerb or less if the road is narrow or within the parking bay lines when parking;

- ► judge when you should begin to straighten up your steering as you enter the side road or parking bay;
- ► correct positioning errors;
- ► deal correctly with other road users;
- ► recognise when you have reversed far enough into the side road to enable you to safely move off from the right hand side of the road;
- ► remember to fasten your seat belt then move off safely from the right hand side of the road;
- ► complete the exercise on sharp and curved corners on roads with varying gradients.

Subject brief

It is often said that reversing to the right is useful when driving a van or similar vehicle. This is because the view to the rear left (i.e. nearside) is restricted.

Vans aren't the only vehicles that are affected by this problem. Many modern sports cars have severely restricted rear vision.

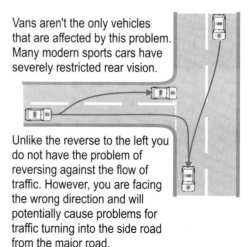

Unlike the reverse to the left you do not have the problem of reversing against the flow of traffic. However, you are facing the wrong direction and will potentially cause problems for traffic turning into the side road from the major road.

The additional learning points that you need to consider with this manoeuvre are:

1. Seating and hand position

When reversing to the right while negotiating the corner you may

need to turn in your seat slightly to the right so that you can look over your right hand shoulder. Your hand position may also switch so that you can use the pull-push method of steering.

The seating and hand position when not negotiating the corner will be the same as when you were reversing in a straight line.

2. All round awareness

You need to take extra care to watch for vehicles from behind that want to turn into the side road. Check through your left (nearside) door mirror and over your left shoulder as necessary. Similarly you will need to particularly watch for oncoming traffic that wants to turn into the side road. As you turn the front of your vehicle will swing out therefore you need to consider whether this will present a hazard to passing traffic on the major road.

3. Dealing with other road users.

You must always be prepared to wait for oncoming traffic to pass. However, you may sometimes find that oncoming traffic turning into the side road will decide to wait for you in which case you would have to continue with the manoeuvre. You will also need to wait for the vehicles approaching from behind if they intend to turn into the side road or if you are at the point just before you propose to turn knowing that your front end will swing into their path.

4. Distance you need to reverse into the side road

To prevent a potential head on collision with traffic turning into the side road it is important that you reverse far enough back to give them sufficient room to stop and overtake you safely. You also need sufficient room to ensure that you will not become a potential hazard to them as you cross over to the left hand lane. Also before moving off you will need to check over your left shoulder.

Lesson quiz

1. Tick any of the following junctions where you think it would be safe to complete a reverse to the right.

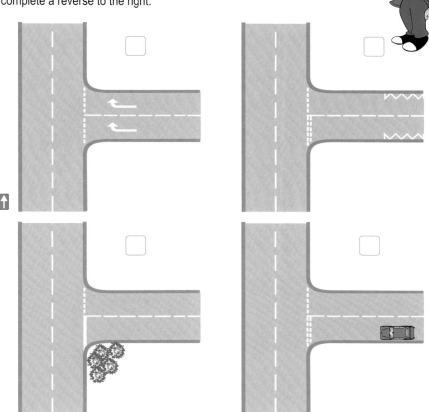

2. The reverse to the right should be used in preference to a reverse to the left:

   ☐ When driving an estate car.

   ☐ When driving a van.

   ☐ When driving any vehicle where your view of the back left hand side or rear window is obscured.

3. What would you do in the following situation? Would you continue with the manoeuvre, pull forward or wait? Assume there are no other vehicles around and that the junctions are open.

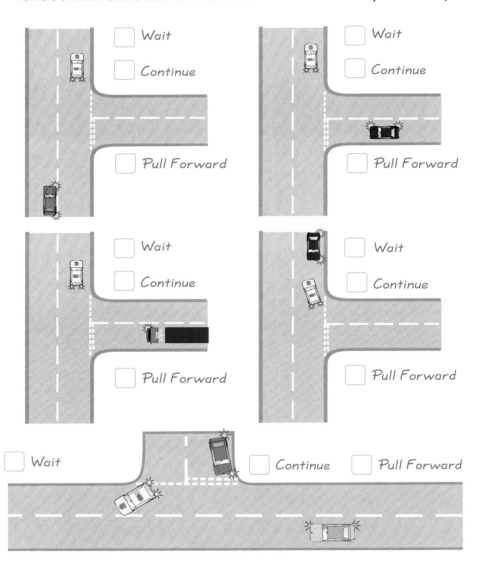

4. After you have reversed into a side road on the right and you want to move back across to the left hand lane which shoulder would you need to look over to check your blind spot.

☐ Left   ☐ Right

5. In the diagram below draw two lines to show the path of the rear wheels of the car as you reverse to the right. Draw boxes to show the points where you would definitely pause to take all round observations and how far you would reverse into the side road before moving over to the left.

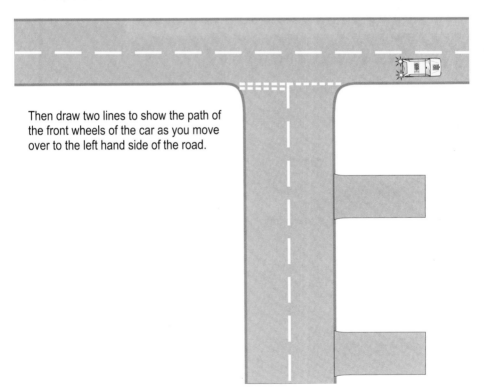

Then draw two lines to show the path of the front wheels of the car as you move over to the left hand side of the road.

Lesson targets

Clutch Control ✓
MSM Routine ✓
...ination ✓

At the end of the lesson tick those targets below that have been achieved.
If any of the targets are ticked as completed with help, review them again after
your next lesson.

	With help from my instructor	Without help from my instructor

Before starting the manoeuvre I:

Carefully consider the safety of the location. ① ①

Move into the starting position safely. ② ②

Whilst reversing to the right I:

Keep my speed down to a slow walking pace. ③ ③

Keep a constant lookout for other vehicles. ④ ④

Give way to other road users and pull forward when
necessary. ⑤ ⑤

Keep within two feet of the kerb. ⑥ ⑥

After reversing to the right I:

Take proper observations before moving back to my
own side of the road. ⑦ ⑦

Introduction

The purpose of the turn in the road manoeuvre is to turn the car to face the opposite direction by using the forward and reverse gears. At this stage in the programme you should have mastered all the component skills that make up this manoeuvre namely; the angle start, reversing to the left and reversing to the right. The key to this manoeuvre is fast steering and slow speed via good clutch control.

Lesson Objectives

By the end of this lesson you should be able to:

► Explain when it would not be safe, legal or convenient to carry out this manoeuvre;

► briskly turn full right lock as you drive the car very slowly towards the far side kerb and then rapidly straighten the wheels just prior to reaching the kerb;

► briskly turn full left lock as you reverse the car very slowly towards the near side kerb and then rapidly straighten the wheels just prior to reaching the kerb;

► repeat the above steps as necessary before completing the final step of the manoeuvre;

► use clutch control to deal with any upward and then downward slope caused by the camber in the road;

► take all round observations before and during each step of the manoeuvre remembering to look over your left and then your right shoulder as you reverse;

► apply the hand brake properly between each step;

► deal correctly with other road users;

► complete the exercise on wide and narrow roads with differing cambers and on roads with occasional traffic.

Subject brief

If you found yourself in a dead end road it might be the only manoeuvre that you could use to turn around safely.

The start of the turn (i.e. point 'A') is similar to an 'angle-start'. As you move across to point 'B', you will be using clutch-control to maintain a slow, safe speed and using your observation skills to keep a look out all around for other vehicles.

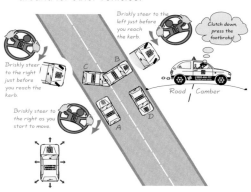

After you have stopped at point 'B', you will reverse to the left (after a slight uphill start). Finally, moving off from point 'C' you will again do a slight uphill start using the same observation and speed control that you would use when emerging from a narrow road to turn right.

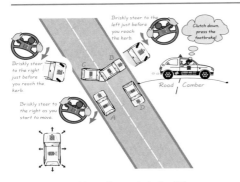

The additional learning points for this manoeuvre are as follows:

1. Location

   Choose a location that is quiet and where you have as much room as possible. Avoid locations where there are trees or posts or other obstructions near or on the kerb. Keep away from parked vehicles and ensure that you will be easily seen by approaching traffic. Once your vehicle is broad side across the road (i.e. in positions B or C in the earlier diagram) you are very vulnerable to approaching traffic from either direction.

2. Steering

   Being able to briskly change the lock of the steering wheel just before you reach point B and point C is the key to completing the manoeuvre in as few movements as possible.

3. Handbrake and clutch control

   The camber of the road may require you to apply the handbrake at point B and C to prevent the car from rolling forward and backwards respectively. It will also require you to use your previously learnt clutch control and braking skills.

4. All round awareness

   All round observations are particularly important to this manoeuvre as you need to be aware of traffic approaching from either side of your vehicle while watching for pedestrians who might cross from the front or the rear. Therefore when you are moving forward you are continually looking from side to side while looking ahead. When reversing you continually move from looking over your left shoulder to your right shoulder as appropriate.

5. Dealing with other vehicles

The manoeuvre should not be started until the road is clear of traffic in both directions. Once you have completed the first leg any traffic that has accumulated can pass behind you if they want to, before you start the second leg. Similarly before commencing the third leg you can allow any traffic that has accumulated to pass in front of you if they want to. The same would apply if it took further movements forwards and backwards to complete the manoeuvre.

6. Number of movements needed

It may not always be possible to complete the manoeuvre in three legs or movements. Additional movements forward and backwards may be needed particularly if the road is very narrow. The procedure for these additional movements is basically the same.

Lesson quiz

1. It might not always be possible to complete the turn-in-the-road in three moves. The number of moves required will depend upon:
    (Tick the relevant answers.)

    ☐ The width of the road.

    ☐ The drivers ability at this manoeuvre.

    ☐ The length of the car.

    ☐ The mood of the driving test examiner.

    ☐ The weight of the car.

    ☐ The steering lock of the car.

2. During the turn-in-the-road show which way you would briskly turn the steering wheel just prior to reaching the kerb at point 'a' and point 'b'.

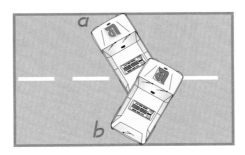

3. When doing the turn in the road manoeuvre you may need to overcome the effects of 'camber'. Mark the diagram below, to show where this driver would control the speed, using:

    a: Clutch-control.
    b: The foot brake.

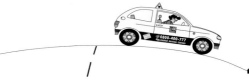

4. The diagram below shows the turn-in-the-road manoeuvre. Three steps towards completion of the manoeuvre have been identified and marked 1 to 3 on the diagram. Number the statements 1 to 3 to match each step of the manoeuvre.

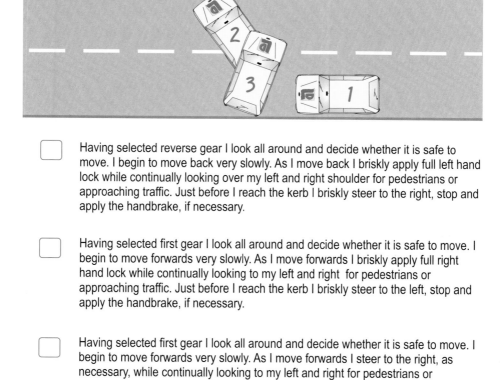

Having selected reverse gear I look all around and decide whether it is safe to move. I begin to move back very slowly. As I move back I briskly apply full left hand lock while continually looking over my left and right shoulder for pedestrians or approaching traffic. Just before I reach the kerb I briskly steer to the right, stop and apply the handbrake, if necessary.

Having selected first gear I look all around and decide whether it is safe to move. I begin to move forwards very slowly. As I move forwards I briskly apply full right hand lock while continually looking to my left and right for pedestrians or approaching traffic. Just before I reach the kerb I briskly steer to the left, stop and apply the handbrake, if necessary.

Having selected first gear I look all around and decide whether it is safe to move. I begin to move forwards very slowly. As I move forwards I steer to the right, as necessary, while continually looking to my left and right for pedestrians or approaching traffic. I then check my mirrors and drive on, if safe.

Lesson targets

At the end of the lesson tick those targets below that have been achieved.
If any of the targets are ticked as completed with help, review them again after your next lesson.

	With help from my instructor	*Without help from my instructor*

Before starting the turn-in-the-road I:

Carefully consider the safety of the location. ① ①

Make sure that the road is clear and that there is sufficient time for at least the first leg of the turn. ② ②

When turning I:

Keep my speed down to a slow walking pace. ③ ③

Keep a constant look out for other vehicles. ④ ④

Give way to other road users when necessary. ⑤ ⑤

Take full and effective observation before each leg of the turn. ⑥ ⑥

After turning around I:

Pull up, or drive on safely, taking care not to inconvenience other road users. ⑦ ⑦

M5 - Reverse Parking

Introduction

The reverse park is an essential skill to learn if you want to be able to park in town on the street. More often than not there is insufficient space to drive forward into a vacant parking space and therefore your only option is to reverse in.

Lesson Objectives

By the end of this lesson you should be able to:

- ► Explain when it would not be safe, legal or convenient to carry out this manoeuvre;

- ► pull up in a suitable position along side the car you intend to park behind and immediately select reverse gear to warn other road users of your intentions;

- ► explain the dangers that the car presents as you undertake this manoeuvre;

- ► judge when you can begin to turn to the left and straighten the wheels to enable you to reverse the car towards the kerb at an angle of 45 degrees;

- ► make effective observational checks throughout the manoeuvre and especially before you turn, ensuring it is safe to proceed;

- ► judge when you can begin to steer to the right and straighten the wheels to enable you to reverse the car along side and parallel to the kerb;

- ► deal correctly with other road users;

- ► complete the manoeuvre within two car lengths from the back of the parked vehicle in front and less than half a metre from the kerb.

Subject brief

The reverse park manoeuvre requires you to pull along side the target vehicle you propose to park behind.

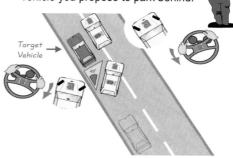

Target Vehicle

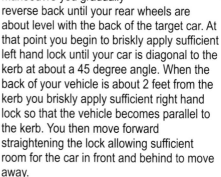

Then having checked that it is safe to commence the manoeuvre you gradually reverse back until your rear wheels are about level with the back of the target car. At that point you begin to briskly apply sufficient left hand lock until your car is diagonal to the kerb at about a 45 degree angle. When the back of your vehicle is about 2 feet from the kerb you briskly apply sufficient right hand lock so that the vehicle becomes parallel to the kerb. You then move forward straightening the lock allowing sufficient room for the car in front and behind to move away.

On the driving test although you are not required to move forward (as there will not be a vehicle behind you) it is acceptable to do so provided you can still pull away from behind the vehicle in front without having to reverse again. Irrespective of this the manoeuvre must be done within two car lengths of the rear of the target vehicle in front.

The additional learning points associated with this manoeuvre are as follows.

1. Location
   Carefully assess the parking space to ensure it is at least one and a half car lengths in size and that it is safe, legal and convenient.

2. Signal your intentions clearly
   Make sure your intentions are known by slowing down well before the parking space and by positioning yourself reasonably close and parallel to the vehicle that you intend to park behind. Immediately get ready to reverse. The brake and reversing lights become a signal to following traffic.

3. Target car position
   Try to position your car parallel to the target vehicle such that it will allow sufficient room for oncoming vehicles to

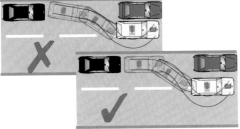

pass or following vehicles to overtake but not so close that it prevents you from completing the manoeuvre in the space available. The closer you are to the target car the more difficult it will be to get a suitable angle to reverse into the space available.

4. All round awareness
   Particularly watch out for pedestrians from either side of the road who may cross behind you as you attempt to reverse . This will require you to be continually looking over your left and right hand shoulder being careful to pause using clutch control when your view to the rear is temporarily lost in the switch over. Check that you will not present a hazard to passing vehicles as your vehicle swings out. Similarly ensure you will not hit the rear of the target vehicle with the front of your car as you swing in.

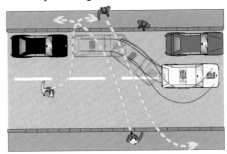

5. Dealing with other road users
   You must always give way to other road users. You must give way to any pedestrians crossing behind and avoid swinging the car out into the path of overtaking or oncoming vehicles.

6. Keeping calm

Other experienced drivers will appreciate that if you rush this manoeuvre you will end up taking longer and run the risk of hitting something or someone. Therefore if traffic appears once you have started the manoeuvre you will usually find that they give you priority. Under no circumstances allow yourself to be hurried when doing this exercise.

Parking in bays

When parking in a bay or reversing into a driveway you will use the same basic reversing skills as when reversing to the left or right. As you will probably be parking in a busy car park it is vitally important that your observations are effective and you keep the speed of your vehicle down to a very slow walking pace. Remember that pedestrians use car parks as well and may walk in front of or behind your vehicle.

Choose the bay you want to reverse into and pull up about 2 car lengths past it at right angles to the white lines. Select reverse gear, take good all round observations to make sure it is safe to move, then reverse back until the first white line of the bay you are reversing into appears to be in line with the top of the back seat, (just as the kerb does when reversing around a corner). At this point take all round observations again, then, if it is safe to do so, steer full lock as the car moves slowly backwards into the bay. As the car becomes straight and parallel with the first white line straighten up the steering and continue to reverse into the bay adjusting the steering as appropriate in order to finish parked straight and centrally between the two white lines.

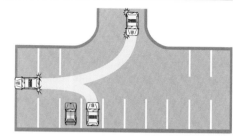

If space is limited in the car park it may be necessary to steer to the right as you reach the bay you want to reverse into. This will mean that you will need less steering to actually enter the bay and so the front of your vehicle will need less room to swing out. From this position you will be able to see both whitelines and steer between them, keep glancing in the door mirrors as you go back to make sure that you finish parked straight and centrally between the two white lines.

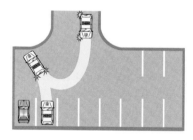

Lesson quiz

1. The diagram below shows the reverse parking manoeuvre. Six steps towards completion of the manoeuvre have been identified and marked 1 to 6 on the diagram. Number the statements 1 to 6 to match each step of the manoeuvre. To help you start, step 1 has been completed for you.

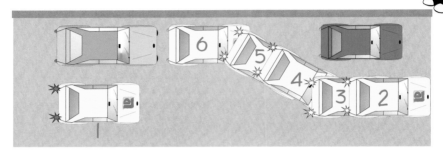

☐ Continue to reverse slowly until the rear wheels of the car are level with the back of the target vehicle then take all round observations to make sure it is safe to commence the next step.

☐ As the rear nearside of the car is about 2 feet from the kerb briskly apply sufficient right hand lock to enable the car to become parallel with the kerb while making sure that there is sufficient room for the front of the car to swing in.

☐ Move forward until you are parallel to and level with, or a little way past, the forward target vehicle stop and prepare to reverse. If safe, commence to reverse in a straight line.

☐ Briskly apply sufficient left hand lock as you move back until the car is diagonal to the kerb then straighten the lock as you continue to reverse back being careful to watch for pedestrians crossing behind from either side of the road.

☐ Stop before you touch the vehicle behind. Slowly move forward straightening the lock leaving sufficient room for the vehicle in front and behind to move off.

1 Slow down as you approach the parking space and ensure that there is sufficient room to park.

2. As you start to do the reverse park manoeuvre in the examples below you notice that a vehicle appears to your rear and stops. What should you do?

☐ Continue   ☐ Beckon them to overtake   ☐ Pull forward

☐ Continue   ☐ Beckon them to overtake   ☐ Pull forward

3. After you have reached the position shown below during the reverse park manoeuvre you notice that a vehicle appears to your front. What should you do?

☐ Continue   ☐ Beckon them to pass   ☐ Pull forward

4. Which of the following pictures show the correct way to bay park

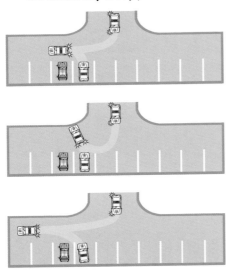

5. After completing the manoeuvre should you be central to the bay markings.

   ☐ Yes   ☐ No

6. If reversing into the bay marked with an X, draw the route you would take and indicate with an R (Right) or L (Left) for which shoulder you would be looking over.

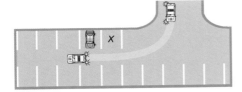

7. As in the previous question, draw your route to park in bay 2 then draw and explain the observations you would make.

Reasons for observations.

M5 - Reverse Parking

Lesson targets

At the end of the lesson tick those targets below that have been achieved.
If any of the targets are ticked as completed with help, review them again after your next lesson.

	With help from my instructor	Without help from my instructor
Before starting the reverse parking manoeuvre I:		
Check that the size of the parking space is sufficient and that the location is suitable.	1	1
Signal my intention to park.	2	2
Move into a suitable starting position.	3	3
When parking I:		
Keep my speed down to a slow walking pace and pause when my view to the rear is obstructed.	4	4
Keep a constant look out for other vehicles and pedestrians.	5	5
Give way to other road users when necessary.	6	6
Park reasonably close and parallel to the kerb.	7	7
Park in the centre of the bay.	8	8
After parking I:		
Move off safely using my angle-start skills.	9	9

Quiz answers

1. Getting Moving
Q1.   L, R, R   C, B, A
Q2.   F, T, T, T
Q3.

Q4.   2
Q5.   T, T, T
Q6.   T, F, T
Q7.   C, A, B, D
Q8.   False
Q9.   ✓ ✗ ✗
Q10.   See Page 7 diagram (Doors).
Q11.   The left hand.
Q12.   ✓ ✗
Q13.   F(medical exceptions), F, T, T
Q14.   ✓ ✗ ✗
Q15.   ✗ ✗ ✓
Q16.   ✓ ✓ ✓ ✓ ✗ T
Q17.   ✗ ✓ ✗
Q18.   ✗ ✓ ✓
Q19.   ✗ ✓ ✓
Q20.   Clutch

Q21.   3, 2, 1
Q22.   1, 3, 2
Q23.   1, 3, 2, 4 or 2, 3, 1, 4
Q24.   2, 1, 3
       7, 5 ,6, 4
Q25.   3, 4, 1
       7, 2, 5, 6
Q26.   See page 8 diagram (observe) and
       page 9 top diagram.
Q27.   See page 9 bottom diagram.

2. Gears
Q1.   5, 2, 3, 1, 4
Q2.   1, 3 5
       2, 4
Q3.   ✗ ✓ ✗
Q4.   No
Q5.   See page 21 top diagram.

3. Steering
Q1.   Third or fourth box
       from the top
Q2.   False
Q3.   ✓ ✗ ✗
Q4.   To the sides, T
Q5.   ✗ ✓ ✗
Q6.   True

4. Co-ordination
Q1.   True
Q2.   B, C, A, D
Q3.   See page 31 second diagram
       from bottom.
Q4.   No
Q5.   See page 31 bottom diagram.
Q6.   1, X, 2
Q7.

Q8.   MSM

5. The emergency stop
Q1. 8.84^m to 9^m, 11.43^m to 12^m,
       14.75^m to 15^m, 17.68^m to 18^m
Q2.   Left
Q3.   30 mph, 40 mph, 50 mph
       Thinking distance, Braking distance.
Q4.   True
Q5.   Both
Q6.   False

6. Hazard drill and basic junctions

Q1. M S P S G or M S P S L
Q2. Yes
Q3. No
Q4.

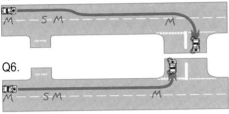

Q5.

Q6.

Q7. See page 30, page 52 Q19 plus your instructor.
Q8. B, X, B, B, B, B, X, R
Q9. 2nd, 1st
Q10. 1st, 2nd
     3rd, 1st
Q11. 1st, 1st
Q12. Brakes
Q13. Yes
Q14. No
Q15. ✗ ✗ ✓
Q16. True
Q17.

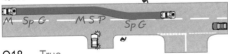

Q18. True
Q19. True
Q20. True
Q21. See yellow boxes on the diagram on page 42.
Q22. Yes
Q23. No
Q24. Yes

Q25.

Q26. C, A, B, E, D
Q27.

Q28. B, R, L, B
Q29. Below where the graph reaches 10mph.
Q30. Below where the graph reaches 5mph.
Q31. Below where the graph reaches 10mph (A) and below where the graph reaches 5mph (B) No.
Q32. True
Q33. C, A, B
Q34. 2nd, 1st
     1st/2nd, 1st
Q35. False
Q36. False
Q37. 1 Left, 1 Right
Q38.

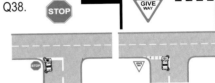

Q39. Left
Q40.

Q41.

Q42. False
Q43. True
Q44.

7. Crossroads

Q1.   None, Yes, Yes
Q2.   Yes
Q3.   Neither, give priority to the green car.
Q4.   Safer, Usual
Q5.   Car A
Q6.   No
Q7.   No
Q8.   Yes
Q9.

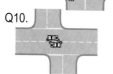

Q10.

8. Emerging from busier Junctions

Q1   ✓ ✗
Q2.   False
Q3.   ✗ ✗ ✓
Q4.   True
Q5.   True
Q6.   Yes, False
Q7.   True
Q8.   ✗ ✗ ✗ ✓

9. Roundabouts

Q1.

Q2.   Yes
Q3.   Yes
Q4.   True
Q5.   True
Q6.   Yes
Q7.   London (L), Conset (L), St Albans (R), Birmingham (C)
Q8.   True
Q9.   ✗ ✓

Q10

Q11.   A=   L   L   -
       B=   L/R   None   1
       C=   R   R   2
       D=   R   R   3
       E=   R   R   4

10. Pedestrians crossings and traffic signals

Q1.   b, c, e, d, b
      b, a, e, d, b
Q2.   e, d, a, b/c
Q3.   ✗ ✓
Q4.   Unmarked
Q5.   ✗ ✓ ✗
Q6.   ✗ ✓
Q7.

Q8.   No
Q9.   No - The crossing is not staggered
Q10. False
Q11. Stop
Q12. ✓ ✗ ✓

II. Hazard perception and defensive driving

Q1. 30mph (13.4^m, 3.35^{cl}),
40mph (17.88^m, 4.47^{cl}),
50mph (22.36^m, 5.59^{cl}),
60mph (26.8^m, 6.70^{cl}),

Q2. ✗ ✗ ✓
Q3. ✗ ✓ ✗
Q4. ✓ ✗ ✗
Q5. ✗ ✗ ✓
Q6. True
Q7. ✓ ✓ ✓ ✗ ✓ ✓
Q8. A = behind line 2, B = behind line 4
Q9. T, T, F, T, F, T, F, T, F
Q10. ✗ ✓
Q11. Hazard lights
Q12. ✗ ✓ ✗
Q13. Ball; Young child on corner; Unmarked side roads left and right.
Q14. ✓ ✗ ✗
Q15. Wait

I2. Dual carriageways

Q1. a, b
Q2. F, F, T, T
Q3.

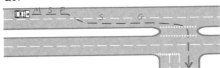

Q4. See page 108 bottom diagram.
Q5. b
Q6. (X) near start of red line.
Q7. False
Q8. To the centre of the lane.
Q9. 1, 3
Q10. True
Q11. ✗ ✓ ✓
Q12. ✗ ✗ ✓

Q13. W, G, G, G, W
Q14. ✗ ✗ ✗ ✓
Q15. 1
Q16. 4
Q17. ✓ ✗ ✗
Q18. Slip road
Q19. Insufficient space to stop halfway

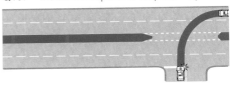

Q20. 30 - 70?, 30 min, 40 max, 70 max

I3. Town and city centre driving

Q1. b
Q2. ✗ ✓
Q3. 1, X, 2, X, 3
Q4. Yes
Q5. Contra-flow bus lane.
Q6. Stop just before side road on left.
Q7. ✗ ✓
Q8.

Q9. ✗ ✓
Q10. X, Y/W, X, X

I4. Progressive driving

Q1. ✗ ✗ ✓ ✗
Q2. ✓ ✗ ✓ ✗ ✓ ✗
Q3. 60 mph
Q4. B, B, A
Q5.

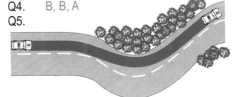

Quiz answers

Q6   Wet Leaves.
Q7.   A) Yes, but not advisable, B) No
Q8.   Overtake
Q9.   Overtake with extreme
      care
Q10.

Q11.   C,
         B, A
Q12.   ✓ ✗ ✗

MI. Straight line reversing
Q1.   ✗ ✗ ✓ ✗ ✓
Q2.   True
Q3.   12 O'clock position, Right
Q4.

Q5.   b
Q6.   B, A, C
Q7.   C, A, B

M2. Reversing to the left
Q1.   ✗ ✓ ✗
Q2.   2, a, 3, c, b
       O = At start; just before turn; just
       after turn.
Q3.   side road, main road,
       reversing.
Q4.   Top left =   Wait
       Top right =   Wait
       Bottom left = Pull forward
       Bottom right =Pull forward

M3. Reversing to the right
Q1.   Top = ✗ ✗
       Bottom = ✓ ✓
Q2.   ✗ ✓ ✓
Q3.   Top = Wait, Wait.
       Middle = Pull forward, Continue.
       Bottom = Pull forward.
Q4.   Left
Q5.

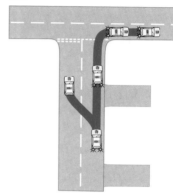

M4. Turn in the road
Q1.   ✓ ✓ ✓ ✗ ✗ ✓
Q2.   a = Left, b = Right.
Q3.

Q4,   2, 1, 3

M5. Reverse parking
Q1.   3, 5
       2, 4
       6, 1
Q2.   Continue, Pull forward.
Q3.   Continue.
Q4.   a and b
Q5.   Yes

Q6

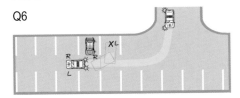

Q7

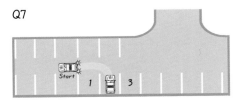

All round observations are neccesary
throughout the manoeuvre to ensure a safe
passage into the parking bay.

What now - I've passed !

Passing the L test is just the beginning. It means you have achieved a minimum level of competency. It does not mean you are an expert. Your hazard perception, defensive driving and progressive driving skills will take time and effort to perfect. Sadly, most drivers who pass the test allow their driving skills to deteriorate. They become over confident and complacent. They rely on reactions rather than forward planning. They become very much like the superman and superwoman depicted in Lesson 11.

Take Pass Plus training

Because your progressive and motorway driving skills are not specifically tested on the normal driving test the Driving Standards Agency have introduced a training scheme called Pass Plus. This scheme involves you in taking extra hours of training with an Approved Driving Instructor. Upon receipt of this training you will be awarded a certificate which entitles you to a reduction in motor insurance premiums. Please note not all motor insurance companies recognize this scheme. Your driving instructor should be able to provide you with further details.

Become an advanced driver

To become an advanced driver you have to pass an advanced driving test. The best known and probably the most highly regarded test is that offered by the Institute of Advanced Motorists (IAM). Many insurance companies grant substantial discounts to IAM members. The IAM motto is "Skill with responsibility". You may be able to obtain training for this test from your driving instructor or failing that from the local IAM group.

The Royal Society for the Prevention of Accidents (RoSPA) operates a similar group called the RoSPA Advanced Drivers Association. Unlike the IAM test the RoSPA test has three grades gold, silver, and bronze. Again passing this test qualifies you for motor insurance discounts.

Both the IAM and RoSPA advanced driving tests are based on the police system of car control. The basics of which are covered as part of the Learner Driving training programme. We would highly recommend that you acquire Roadcraft The Police Driver's Handbook as part of your preparation for either of these tests. The IAM also have their own manual entitled Pass Your Advanced Driving Test.

An alternative to the above tests is that offered by the Driving Instructors Association. The DIAmond Advanced Motorist test is very similar to the driving test taken by actual driving instructors and is based on part 2 of the DSA's driving instructors qualifying examination. Again motor insurance discounts are available to those who pass the test.

What now - I've passed !

Appointment record

Instructor Details:

Name: _____

School Name: _____

Address: _____

_____

_____

_____

Telephone Numbers:

Home: _____ Mobile: _____

Date	Day	Time	Hours Booked	Hours Taken	Amount £ Paid	Hours Due	Instructors Signature

Appointment record

Date	Day	Time	Hours Booked	Hours Taken	Amount £ Paid	Hours Due	Instructors Signature